Timing is everything, and when I heard that Steve was writing a book to share his story and business success secrets, I was delighted and excited to read it. This book arrives at a time when more people in history are searching for new avenues to reinvent and pursue their dream of owning a business that serves them, not enslaves them. This book is not only inspirational; it's valuable and real. Steve has the expertise and proof to back up his teachings, and I'm certain his book will change lives worldwide for the better. Thanks, Steve, for the gift of your wisdom and passion to help others, which visibly shines through the pages of your wonderful new book!

—TONY RUBLESKI
#1 Best-Selling Author, Speaker, and Cons
www.MindCaptureGroup.com

There are many components needed to succeed as an entrepreneur. Without question, it is passion that is the most import ingredient to serve others and achieve prosperity. Read this book today and learn how you too can harness your passions to achieve prosperity and become an unstoppable entrepreneur!

—PATRICK SNOW
International Best-Selling Author of
Creating Your Own Destiny and *The Affluent Entrepreneur*

Passion drives everything! It motivates you to action. It gets you through the tough times. It inspires you when you get down. It gives reason to what you do and it encourages others. Nothing is more powerful than passion. I would encourage every entrepreneur to read this book and understand the power of passion. Let Steve help you implement this powerful tool in your business. When you get it, I mean, really get it, you will find things get clearer, business gets easier, and it is fun. Steve Adams gets it. He gets it big time. So should you. Read this book!

—RON FINKLESTEIN
International Author of *49 Marketing Secrets (THAT WORK) to Grow Sales*, *The Platinum Rule for Small Business Mastery*, and creator of the businessgrowthexperience.net

I was truly inspired as Steve Adams led me through his entrepreneurial journey and revealed his strategically focused passion for his business and the people most important to him. I remained riveted as he shared his magnificent forward-thinking leadership and turned turmoil and fear into abundance and confidence.

I have had the honor of sharing a small part of the journey Steve Adams has gone through to reach his current success, and I have been truly inspired by his passion. With every meeting, with every conversation, Steve imparts knowledge and wisdom that can only come from an accomplished entrepreneur that has been in the thick of fear and turmoil and then stepped back to focus on the most important elements of life. I encourage you to partake in his wisdom by reading The Passionate Entrepreneur *so you can close the last page of the book enlightened by this path to entrepreneurial success.*

—WALTER BERGERON
Entrepreneur and Author, *The Million Dollar Total Business Transformation*, Winner of the GKIC 2012 National Marketer of the Year award

Steve Adams has put together an amazing book that clearly shows his passion for entrepreneurship. It provides the reader a boost of confidence and "can do" power that will help overcome the obstacles we all face in business and in life. I know that one of the things his company does is "helps leaders develop a positive mindset." Well, he has done a great job in transferring that directly into these pages. In reading this, you can't help but be changed for the better, whether you're a current entrepreneur or thinking about making the jump.

—HENRY EVANS
Author, *The Hour a Day Entrepreneur*, San Diego, CA

The Passionate Entrepreneur *brilliantly lays out the importance of having passion and purpose in your business, balanced with a solid "roll up your sleeves" road map of how to turn your passion into a reasonable business. Steve pulls you in with compelling stories of victory and defeat and how to respond to challenging situations creatively. This book is a must read for any entrepreneur or business professional.*

—DAVE "THE SHEF" SHEFFIELD
Motivational Keynote Speaker and Author of
Blabvertising: The Art of Word-of-Mouth Advertising

Steve Adams' book provides great insights about building a business with passionate employees and devoted customers who go out of their way to do business with you. If you run a business, this book will be an invaluable asset.

—TOM "TOO TALL" CUNNINGHAM
Napoleon Hill Certified Instructor

Steve Adams has built an incredible business by harnessing the power of passion. I appreciate how transparent he is in this book. Passion fueled him to go the extra mile when times were tough. Passion drove him to take massive action. In sharing the story of his own journey, he demonstrated how passion made up for shortcomings in talent and resources and provided the emotional connection that has made his company stand out from the crowd. You'll gain some great insights by reading this book. One of my favorite tips is "how something as simple as shifting your language from 'customer' to 'client' can advance your mission, purpose and vision throughout you entire company." Thank you, Steve, for sharing your story and great wisdom with us!

—KATHY PAAUW
Business and Personal Coach, Entrepreneur,
Author of *The Music of Your Heart*

The
PASSIONATE
ENTREPRENEUR

Essential Building Blocks for
Entrepreneurial Success

STEVE ADAMS

The challenges of being an entrepreneur are similar in all industries. Our community of entrepreneurs can help you grow and be encouraged in your journey.

Scan the QR code below and receive a free educational gift from me. Sign up to become a member of our passionate entrepreneur community.

www.steveadamsbook.com/paperback

Published by Advantage, Charleston, South Carolina.
Member of Advantage Media Group.

ADVANTAGE is a registered trademark and the Advantage colophon is a trademark of Advantage Media Group, Inc.

Printed in the United States of America.

ISBN: 978-1-59932-358-9
LCCN: 2013934810

This publication is designed to provide accurate and authoritative information in regard to the subject matter covered. It is sold with the understanding that the publisher is not engaged in rendering legal, accounting, or other professional services. If legal advice or other expert assistance is required, the services of a competent professional person should be sought.

Advantage Media Group is proud to be a part of the Tree Neutral® program. Tree Neutral offsets the number of trees consumed in the production and printing of this book by taking proactive steps such as planting trees in direct proportion to the number of trees used to print books. To learn more about Tree Neutral, please visit **www.treeneutral.com**. To learn more about Advantage's commitment to being a responsible steward of the environment, please visit **www.advantagefamily.com/green**

Advantage Media Group is a publisher of business, self-improvement, and professional development books and online learning. We help entrepreneurs, business leaders, and professionals share their Stories, Passion, and Knowledge to help others Learn & Grow. Do you have a manuscript or book idea that you would like us to consider for publishing? Please visit **advantagefamily.com** or call **1.866.775.1696.**

To Heidi, my wife of twenty-six years. Thank you for being a firelighter in my life and for being a rock of support at every step in our journey together.

Acknowledgments

WRITING THIS BOOK was the realization of a ten-year goal. For many years I sensed it wasn't time to start because I knew deep down I wasn't ready. I needed to learn and experience more. Those experiences and lessons learned over the past thirty years came from my connection to and investment in other people.

I have several people to thank, and while I will share the names of some individuals here, they are by no means the only people who have positively influenced me as a person and entrepreneur. I am who I am and where I am because of the people I thank in these pages and countless others whom I have not mentioned. They are as much a part of the creation of this book as I am.

I learned character, goal setting, and my work ethic from my parents, Dave and Jean Adams. I could not have had a better childhood, living in a nice Midwestern town with a mom and a dad home to help me grow and experience life in a positive way. Thanks, Mom and Dad, for that.

Ed and Pam Babbitt, the parents of my wife, Heidi, taught me a lot about being a Main Street entrepreneur as they ran their growing power-sports and recreational-vehicle dealership, "selling fun," as Ed liked to say. Thanks for being an encouragement as we pondered starting the business in those tough early years.

I am grateful to my wife, Heidi, and children, Lindsay and Collin. They always have been enthusiastic about our business, welcomed me home joyfully from each business trip, and never complained when there was more month than money. Entrepreneurs need spouses who get it, and I won the lottery with Heidi. She never doubted me or complained. She simply dealt with what she had to work with, made it work and made it fun.

My dad taught me from a young age the phrase, "Readers are leaders." I am grateful to the countless authors who have put their best into a book and provided opportunities for someone like me to learn from them. Authors John Maxwell, Dan Kennedy, Lee Milteer, Richard Koch, Daniel Goleman, Chester Elton, Daniel Pink, Marcus Buckingham, and Jim Collins are a few who had a major impact on my development.

I also want to thank Doug and Sherry Bennett for introducing me to leadership as a path of study and encouraging me when we made our first big move to Wisconsin. Thanks for continuing to invest in me over the past twenty years.

Tom O'Brien, Mike Mueller, Eric Strattan and Tom Watkins have been the best of friends over the past twenty years. Thanks, guys, for all your encouragement at our early morning breakfasts when I didn't know if I was going to make it. Thanks for celebrating our growth today in the same way.

I appreciate Denis, Bob, Brooke, Adam, Patti, and Alison at Advantage Media Group. They helped craft the message, pushed me to complete the content on time, and be flexible with ideas as we progressed through the project. They have a very unique and author-friendly vision at Advantage, and all new authors should look to them to publish their first and any future books.

I want to thank Harvey Solway, former CEO of Pet Supplies Plus, who gave me my first opportunity in business and who was encouraging and helpful as I ran across the potholes of my early business mistakes.

This book wouldn't have been written without the strong support and talents of my primary business partners, Chad Bush and Aaron Young. Without them, we would still have just a few stores. Thanks for your talents, guys, and for the ability you give me to focus on what I am best at.

Finally, I want to thank my PSP team in all twenty-one stores. Space won't allow me to name you all, but you are the people who each day live our vision and the principles of this book. You make the choice every day to go the extra mile with passion to serve our clients and help them have a stress-free pet-ownership experience. I am grateful to all of you.

—STEVE ADAMS, Muskegon, Michigan

Contents

Foreword

IF YOU ARE READING THIS BOOK, *The Passionate Entrepreneur*, by Steve Adams, most likely you are trying to find your passion or light a fire under your passion, and you have found the right book! Nothing is more important or more powerful than the energy of passion to achieve great things on earth.

To be outrageously successful, education is important; work ethic and connections are important, but the energy of passion is the big secret. Passion gets you through all the obstacles and challenges that life and business will present you with to achieve your goals and purpose on earth. Without passion, your life becomes side tracked with an endless to-do list and the feeling of no time or joy for yourself. Most people have not been educated or programmed to make passion a priority in life. The average person spends his or her life living out someone else's dream for so-called security. Truly successful people must know their true calling and align their career with that passion. Unless you take the time and effort to discern what your passion is, mostly likely you will never be able to achieve true happiness or feel fulfilled. To be truly happy in life, you must find that which motivates you. The real you must be unleashed! It doesn't matter what you want to do, as long as it is something that is meaningful and has a power that will propel you through the struggles of your life.

So here are some soul-searching tips to assist you in finding your passion again:

First, read this book cover to cover because the author, Steve Adams, is truly an example of someone who took the road less traveled. Steve, after discovering he had made his family proud by earning an MBA and having a great, secure job with a huge income that others envied, realized all this outside success was not making him happy, and in fact, he felt he was dying inside. Steve had the courage to do what most people simply will not do, which is question his direction, acknowledge his life was not what he wanted, and actually take huge risks to make his life what he wanted. Was it scary? Yes. Did he succeed? Yes, in a huge way. Steve's amazing story will not only motivate you but inspire you with some practical knowledge on how you too can reignite within yourself that spark of fire called passion to make your dreams come true.

To rediscover what your real calling or passion is, ask yourself the following questions:

1. **What is it that makes you smile?**
   Think about the things that you do that put a smile on your face or give you a sense of true belonging.

2. **When does your creativity soar?**
   Your creativity only comes to life if you're inspired, happy, or complete. To find your true passion for life, just look for that one thing that sets your creativity free, that you do with ease and enjoyment. Time flies by when you are involved in this activity.

3. **What are you willing to do for free?**
   When you're doing what you love, you rarely ever think of money. Having real passion for life is about doing that something that you're willing to do without compensation because it makes

you happy. Discovering that passion and converting it into something profitable will help you make money and achieve true happiness.

4. **What do you like to talk about? What topics spark your interest?**

   What is it that you always talk about? If you keep going back to one particular topic no matter what the conversation is and who you're having it with, it's often a sign that topic has something to do with your passion for life. Ask your friends to help you figure this one out.

5. **What kind of reading are your most drawn to?**

   This is a huge hint. It could now be a hobby of yours. What you are putting into your mind and trying to find more information about is a hint.

6. **What are you confident about?**

   When you're trying to revive your passion, you'll have complete confidence in your abilities. Find out that one thing that you do that makes you absolutely unafraid of failure, and you'll be well on your way to discovering your true passion and achieving true happiness.

7. **What is important to me? What would make me happy? What is my higher purpose or passion?**

   To help you answer these questions you first must find your vision. Another important thing to remember is that passion is really another word for vision.

Once you have answered some of these questions you will have some direction on where you should be focusing your energy to fire up your real self and acknowledge your inner passions.

In my career as an author, speaker and entrepreneur coach, I have committed myself to finding ways to assist people to a new mindset that will allow them to take a quantum leap in their lives and businesses by becoming more authentic and using their natural-born talents and passions.

When Steve Adams asked me to write the foreword for *The Passionate Entrepreneur,* I was pleased for many reasons.

Steve is an unbelievably good man who has morals, a great work ethic, and is madly passionate about his businesses, family, and his employees. I met Steve for the first time at my own coaching program called "Peak Performers." I was impressed that the audience was on the edge of their seats when he told his story about how he had broken away from his old successful life, and become an entrepreneur and followed his true passion for entrepreneurship and the pet business. I too am a true animal lover, so I bonded with Steve and his vision right away.

I am happy to report that Steve inspired my entrepreneurial coaching students to realize if they did not have passion for what they were doing, they would only get average incomes. I promise if you follow Steve Adams's advice in this book, you will have a renewed sense of enthusiasm, passion, and vision about the contributions you make to others with your knowledge, products, and services.

So my advice is if you are dreaming of pursuing something different, knowing that dream is coming from inner inspiration and is filled with passion will help to make your big visions a reality. You create your life and legacy daily with the actions you take, thoughts you have, and what you believe to be possible.

I will leave you with these thoughts: Your point of power is this minute in time. When you are formulating your vision, be grand about it; don't think small—think BIG.

—LEE MILTEER
Author, Speaker, Success Coach
www.milteer.com

IN THE
REARVIEW MIRROR

We all have moments fixed in our minds, tableaux that endure time. Let me tell you about two that are forever with me.

It is 1970 and I am six years old. My father is kneeling behind his truck, screwing on the new Michigan license plates. They are yellow and white, not the usual blue. My father grew up in a large, struggling family, the fourth of six children, and he was the first to graduate from high school. He had gone to work in the auto factories, but he wanted more, and later he would go on to get a college degree. As I watch him, he turns suddenly and points a finger at me. Was it something I said? "I'm going to tell you this again," he lectures me. "You are *not* going to work in that #$@ shop. You're going to college, and you're going to use your brain, not your back."

It is 1996 and I am thirty-two years old. The truck is loaded, and I am leaving my wife and two children behind, for now, as I head to Wisconsin to set up our new life. My wife, Heidi, and I spent the evening with our friends Tom and Shelley Watkins and Doug and Sherry Bennett. They came to see us before our move from Muskegon, Michigan, to Appleton, Wisconsin. The Bennetts told us that, years earlier, they moved from Appleton to Muskegon, and their reason was much the same as ours. They had left the comfort of their hometown, their family, and friends to launch a high-risk endeavor. As I turn the ignition to leave, I know that we too are facing a big risk. I look in the rearview mirror and see them all waving, and my heart aches. My wife too feels conflicted. Her family's roots here go back a hundred years, and she is in her dream home with two small children, nine months old and two years old. What am I *thinking*? Am I doing right by my family?

Nobody in my own family, going back generations, had worked in anything other than blue-collar jobs. We did not live the privileged and refined life. Years later, my wife would have to teach me the etiquette of dining at a business meeting. I had no clue.

But I would go on to follow the advice of my father, Dave Adams, as I went from high school to college to a white-collar banking career. By age thirty-two, I was a vice president of corporate banking, a secure job with a great income. I had my MBA. Everyone was proud of me.

And I was dying inside.

I'd done all the things I was supposed to do. I had gone to college, got married, had kids, bought a nice house, and pursued a career at a Fortune 500 company. But as I matured professionally, I realized I was built to create, innovate, and to lead and develop people. I had a passion to be an entrepreneur. I couldn't pursue that in the regulated world of banking, and I feared that if I did not break away, I would lose my passion for work and life.

I had attained a high position in banking at a young age and had a reputation for being entrepreneurial in my approach, aggressive and strategic in prospecting for new business. One of my early mentors, Jim Tomczyk, had told me that if I wanted to go places in banking,

I needed to improve the bottom line by bringing in accounts. Throughout my decade in banking, I studied and networked and fearlessly made cold calls. I brought in a large movie theater and radio station operator as clients, not the norm for a Detroit-based bank that generally dealt with the automotive industry.

With regard to that movie theater account, I had been working for a year on the Chicago deal when I got a call at home one day, telling me that our chief credit officer in Detroit wanted major changes made to the deal. I was upset; I had devoted so much time to it. I ended up getting the deal done, but it wasn't fun. The system was killing my motivation and innovative spirit. How could I do this for the rest of my life? The thought gripped me.

"I think I am just going to go start a McDonald's in North Dakota," I told a friend as we sat at a Burger King in downtown Grand Rapids, "and get out of this industry." I was willing to accept probably one of the few remaining territories available for a McDonald's franchise in a remote area over continuing in a job and industry for which I no longer had a passion. At least there, I would have an opportunity to grow and use my skills in a business.

"Don't do that," my friend said. "My dad owns a Pet Supplies Plus. Why don't we look at doing that?" Initially we considered partnering, but ultimately he chose not to pursue the business while I made the decision to move forward. And that started my journey toward being an entrepreneur. That was 1995. As of this writing, my two operating partners and I now have twenty-one franchised stores. We have plans to open multiple stores annually over the next several years.

Pet Supplies Plus had been in business since 1988. The three main pet-supply chains in America today all started the superstore format in 1988. PetCo was a chain of small stores in California that migrated to the big format. PetSmart was started from scratch by a Harvard graduate who observed the industry and began with a big-store format in Phoenix, Arizona.

The owner and founder of Pet Supplies Plus is Jack Berry. He was a lifelong grocer, and he had a vision of a grocery store for pets. He studied the competition and envisioned a smaller store that would be easier for shopping and could be located near neighborhood grocery stores. He felt that people would buy pet supplies and groceries on the same trip.

Berry believed in franchising. He maintained that he could set up most of what was needed to be successful, but that it was the entrepreneur's innovative portion and passion that made all the difference in the world—and he was right.

The original vision that Berry had was one of self-service. When I got into the business, I agreed with how he had positioned it. But I also felt it could be really special to combine that with a "raving-fans" type of service model, based on the book of that title by Ken Blanchard.

In 1996 there were about seventy-five Pet Supplies Plus stores nationally. Today there are 270, and Pet Supplies Plus ranks among the top pet-specialty retail chains. I came into the business believing that there would be a competitor in every city, and so with our first store, on day one, we started building the culture to face that reality. Back then, there was a lot of space for competition; today, it seems everybody wants to be in the pet business. All the big retail chains sell pet supplies now. You can buy pet supplies online. You can buy pet supplies at home-improvement stores.

I believed the only long-term way to build this business and defend it from competitive forces was to have amazing employees in the store who would build relationships, share the enthusiasm, and develop expertise that could not be replicated by our larger competitors. We would be a company of passionate people who went the extra mile in everything we did.

A Passion for Entrepreneurship

I enjoy pets; our family has a dog named Bella who is a wonderful labradoodle, but it wasn't a passion for animals that brought me into the industry. My motivation and my drive were based on something else. I came at the industry from more of a strategist mindset. One of the things you learn as a banker is how to evaluate healthy industries. It is very important when making loans. It doesn't matter how good a particular business is faring in the short run if the industry is sinking or has been commoditized.

What I liked about the pet-supply industry was the emotional connection: it can be built upon people and on relationships with customers in a way that cannot be copied and commoditized. And I liked that the industry already had three major chains. It wasn't inundated with players all trying their own ways to chase the customer. These were large companies making rational, competitive decisions.

I was getting into a growing industry. When I got into the business in 1996, it was making about $12 billion in revenues, and today it is making about $56 billion. It has been expanding at roughly twice the rate of the U.S. economic growth over the last fifteen years. I could see that this was a business that was raring to grow.

The customers brought with them a natural passion for what we offered them. It was a fit for me, and my passion was to lead and motivate people as an entrepreneur. I had found my niche.

Let me make this clear: There are many niches for success. Another entrepreneur may find a future in industrial fittings. This is not a book for animal lovers, necessarily, nor those interested in the pet product business. It is for readers who harbor another kind of drive: a passion for entrepreneurship.

I am a continuous learner. It is how I am wired. Since childhood, I have had a pattern of risk taking and reaching to accomplish what cannot be done if you play it safe all the time. At age ten, I started my own lawn business. I mowed the yard for several families on my street, and that led me to become a student janitor in high school and take on painting jobs, even though I was playing three sports.

I wanted to play football in college but did not have a scholarship, so I chose a school with a great business program: Northwood University. I made the team there just by walking on, and then I got a scholarship. And while I was studying and playing football—I was a safety—I also started my own painting business during the summers to make extra money.

When I took my first job out of college, I accepted a position at a bank that paid less than others because I felt it would be where I could learn the most. In the first two years, I was a manager trainee at the bank and moved up quickly. I soon saw that if I wanted to be a leader in the bank, I would need to go through the credit training and the corporate banking side. I took a pay-grade reduction in my job classification so that I could make that switch. I knew that in the long run I would rise much further in the bank by doing that.

Such risks paid off, and by that pivotal point in 1996, I was ready for the big change. I had a track record of working through big decisions that involved risk. I took risks as a banker, making choices on which loans I would seek approval for. That is how I made my name as a banker. I would see companies with good management but whose story made other bankers say, "This is not worth it. I do not want to put the work into this deal." But I would put the work in, and understand the business, and get the deal done. That is how I built my portfolio.

By my early thirties I'd worked hard and devoted the time to becoming somebody more than I was when I was twenty-two. I had invested in several personal-growth taped programs, attended seminars, and read probably three hundred books in that decade. My mentor, Doug Bennett, had continually challenged me with new material and thinking and introduced me to Dr. John Maxwell's books and tapes. But I felt as if I could no longer apply what I was learning. Our banking clients were not valuing our work. It was more and more about price. The banking business was becoming commoditized. People just wanted the cheapest rate.

"I can't spend the next thirty years doing this," I thought. "I've got to be somewhere where I can apply what I'm learning." I could still hear my father's advice of so many years earlier: use your brain, not your back. To which I would add: be driven by your passion, not your fears.

I love to develop people and to have a positive influence on their lives. I saw entrepreneurship as an opportunity to do that, and I have had ample opportunity to do so. Our philosophy today toward high-school-age employees, for example, is to teach them skills they can use in their future. I get excited about that. I feel fulfilled when I see a manager's life transformed by working with us.

Getting in the Game

I want to inspire entrepreneurs to have the courage to get in the game and to build the business that they are secretly dreaming about every day. It is a passion that permeates those in the corporate world. In fact, nationally known career coach Lee Milteer found that after she spoke to corporate audiences, many seemed ready to quit their jobs on the spot and strike out on their own. I knew that feeling well.

If you are dreaming of pursuing something different, I want to encourage you that you can do it. Let your vision be big, bigger than just attaining the lifestyle you want, because that is not what inspires. That is just the result. Instead, build a cathedral, as author Michael Feiner says in his book *The Feiner Points of Leadership*. Build an enterprise through which you can inspire others. That is the key. If you are the only one inspired, you have a small vision. The real challenge is creating a vision that inspires not only you but also all of your employees.

Our story is an example of that. This is not a how-to book on building a retail business. That is not my goal here. What I want to do in this book is to tell you what, why, and some of the how. It is up to you to synthesize the information in this book and apply the how to your own business or personal situation. By telling our own story, I want to motivate you to launch your own dream or reimagine the future of the business you are already in. I want to encourage you to pursue what you are yearning to do. I want you to capture the passion that is already inside you.

The growth of businesses and entrepreneurialism is a key component of what makes America work, and you will find, in this book, a lot of advice on business process and good practices. But what runs through every page is passion. This is a book to encourage entrepreneurs to pursue their passions and show them specific and proven ways to do so successfully, particularly by appealing to the passions of their customers or clients.

This is essential for entrepreneurs who want to compete against the giants in their industry, and most industries have them, whether they are selling pet supplies or running shoes. The competition may seem formidable, but you can stand up against anybody if you have a strong strategic vision and the passion to follow through on it. Ingenuity and innovation are the hallmarks of successful entrepreneurs.

In a more entrepreneurial organization, customers and clients get more personal service. The Wal-Marts of the world lower prices via efficiency to build business. Companies like Apple choose the path of product innovation that gives customers something they did not even know they wanted. Our model has been customer intimacy. An entrepreneur's passion for personal service always benefits the consumer or the client. Why? By having a business model that focuses on the clients, you solve their problems or "pain points" and, as a result, fill their needs.

Entrepreneurship is good for the community at large, which benefits from the diversity of enterprise. Across America you will find many communities that have been greatly enriched by a family enterprise. In Michigan, not far north of our headquarters, the Gerber baby food company has helped the town of Fremont thrive. In Grand Rapids, the two families that built Amway have invested tens of millions of dollars into hospitals and charities and the downtown landscape. Many towns have such a story, and it is not necessarily one big, famous company that has worked the magic. A community may have thirty well-run businesses that each, in its unique way, has an impact. They pay for a park project or fund a Little League team or support the high-school booster club.

This is good for America. It puts people to work, it pulls in tax revenue, and it keeps the economic engines pumping. The impact is massive. It is often pointed out how banks multiply money: for every dollar of your deposit, a bank can lend out ten dollars because it only needs to reserve approximately 10 percent. The reality is that banks do not multiply the money. They simply are the conduit for multiplication. It is the entrepreneurs of America who use that money to do something productive.

Our country needs men and women with a vision and a willingness to take risk, stand in line, and accept that money and create something new from it. We need more such visionaries. As a commercial lender for a bank, I saw how too much money chased too few quality deals. We need the entrepreneur's brainpower. We need a diversity of businesses. When they thrive, they employ people and generate tax revenue that gets reinvested in roads and utilities and the infrastructure of a thriving economy.

Over the past five years I have participated in microfinance projects in Russia, Serbia, Jordan, and now, Central Asia. The goal of these projects is to launch businesses that will stand out and grow by investing in people and caring for them. While working on these projects, I have seen corruption and a lack of a good legal system. Sometimes bribery is the name of the game. There are few protections for intellectual property. Businesses lack access to good capital markets, and university research is lacking.

By contrast, America has a great playing field. Our government, despite what some might think of it, is stable and provides an environment that helps entrepreneurs build the businesses of their dreams. We must strive to make sure it stays that way. What we need to do is get more people in the game. When we encourage that, we encourage a cycle of reinvestment in our communities. Government doesn't build our businesses; we do. However, we must recognize the role that government plays in providing the building blocks to effective enterprise.

We need to see more people pursuing their entrepreneurial dreams. I want to offer whatever I can to help that happen. I want to do what I can to nurture the spirit of ingenuity that I hope will always define us. Together, we can multiply our resources to keep our economy strong.

In a recent visit to Baltimore, I marveled at the shipyards as I drove up I-95. I thought of the many generations it took to build that industrial base, that infrastructure. I thought of all the entrepreneurs who took so many risks to make that happen. When you consider that Baltimore is just one community among many thousands across the nation, you can see the sheer power of our creative spirit. It is the fuel of our economic engine. It is the power behind our government, our military, our entire political and social system. Without the entrepreneurs who create wealth, we would be nothing. Our government and military would be powerless, our schools ineffectual. Everything stagnates without the innovation of the entrepreneurs who create fundamental value.

In *Atlas Shrugged*, Ayn Rand posed the question of what would happen if all the entrepreneurs just gave up out of frustration. We need to pay attention to the fundamentals that drive our economy. Otherwise, we face collapse.

It Is All in the Trajectory

Business has been fun for me lately, and that is because our business connects with people. They appreciate our brand. I have a good relationship with a great and dedicated team that goes above and beyond for our clients, who have sent us numerous testimonials. I have wonderful partners who complement me with strengths I do not have. Without them our organization would not be where it is today. Our franchise system and its leadership are talented and innovative and aggressive. As an entrepreneur, it isn't all about me; it is about having a great team and a network of support.

Today we are experiencing double-digit, year-over-year sales growth in those stores that have been open at least one year. We recently opened several more stores in anticipation of doubling the company size within a few years. Our profitability is strong and rapidly increasing. Each store has a team of people who are trained and passionate about pets and serving people. We are aligned around a common purpose and mission.

Business is fun when you are on an upward trajectory. It is not that I am free of debt and have no problems. Rather, I know that all the pieces are in place, and every day I am excited to wake up. I enjoy the people I work with, and we have positive momentum. That is what makes it fun.

I have endured less-than-joyous times. I have made mistakes, and I learned valuable lessons from them. By sharing my story, I hope to help you steer clear of those mistakes , or at least to encourage you through your own challenges. I want to encourage you to pursue your business with passion, because, come what may, that is what gets you through. Without passion, you will not persist.

In the spring of 1998, two years into my business, I opened a second location too soon. We would have been all right except that a major new national pet chain moved into town six months after our store opening. When that chain arrived, our sales dropped 30 percent. I had already been losing money but had been able to manage it. Now, I was losing a lot of money. I could see that in two months, it would all come to an end if I didn't boldly act.

I remember thinking that I just wanted to quit. Two years earlier, I had been personally debt free, with a nice income and a promising banking career. But then I recalled how I had been dying inside. I had been led out of Egypt, so why was I clamoring to go back? I had started this business to make a difference. I had set out to build something great. What I needed was to buy more time. I needed to return to operating out of vision rather than fear.

Only a day after I had those thoughts, the bank that had financed my business called me and asked me to consider coming out of banking retirement and working for its organization. It was a hard decision. Would I be demonstrating a lack of commitment and faith if I left the business to go back to work in banking? Should I just stay and figure it out that way? The stress was palpable.

I told Heidi that I was going to give her a break, and I would take our kids—they were two and four years old then—to visit the Yogi Bear Campground in northern Wisconsin for the weekend. I was going to figure out whether I should stay in the business, or go back into banking.

I played with the kids all day and then put them to bed in the cabin around eight o'clock. I sat by the fire for four hours, staring into the flames. I prayed, and I meditated on Proverbs 3: 5–6, and at about midnight I found peace. I realized that I had a deep desire to keep my business going and that I would not quit. But I had been given an opportunity to work while continuing to operate the business and fix my financial problems. It would benefit no one if I ran out of cash and failed.

So that is what I did. I went back into banking for four years. I worked two jobs (the business and my bank job) for those four years, but during that time, I was able to clean up all of my mistakes to that point and put us back on stable ground financially, both in the business and at home. I was able to buy time. It kept us going through those early years. Without the passion to keep going, though, I would have quit. I would have folded up the business and gone back into banking and tried to be comfortable.

I needed that time by the fire. I saw my family's future dancing in those flames. I could see that we would endure if we kept the fire going, and if I could remain, as Yogi would put it, "smarter than the average bear."

I would go back into banking, yes, and do what I must, but nothing was going to dim my passion for entrepreneurship. I had heard the same advice so many times: "Just follow your dreams and passions, and the money will follow." I don't subscribe to that philosophy. I argue throughout this book that indeed passion is at the core of success. However, all successful entrepreneurs and people in general have to do work they don't like, or work through circumstances in a fashion that is not their passion, to be able to continue with what they love. The money isn't automatic if you just follow your dreams. Financial success involves a lot of difficult and tough work and enduring seemingly endless obstacles and adversity.

I recalled how I had felt as I pulled away in the packed truck, off to start my business, and saw my family waving as I looked through the rearview mirror. I could have turned around and gone back into their arms and back to what was comfortable. I could have flown back to safety, never to find excitement, and I recalled the flush of adrenaline and energy I felt once I was driving up the highway.

I resolved that I would not think small—and every entrepreneur battles that tendency, that desire to pull back to an easier life. But the easier life, I knew, would be the hardest on my heart. I would continue the work, and to do the hard stuff I didn't like, because I believed that in the end I would figure it out. I would come up with the answers, get the right people around me, and eventually success would follow.

Finding Your Secret Sauce

As we built our brand for our group of Pet Supplies Plus stores, we knew we wanted one so strong that our clients would drive right on past our competitors' stores and come to us. They would know that what we offered matched what they wanted.

That sounds simple, but it is hard to do well. People care deeply about the family pet When they go out to purchase things for their pet, they do not want to feel as if they are just buying a garden hose or office supplies. They want an experience. That is what they tell us.

We have created a brand in which our clients can have a relationship with our staff. They can have fun when they shop, and they can get an education about pet care as well. We want our clients to feel confident that they are doing all they can for their pets.

By communicating a desire to help, you are communicating that you care about more than simply making a buck. You care about the quality of your clients' experience with your brand. For us, that means helping them care for their pets. After all, most pet owners define their pets as members of the family.

Consumers these days have low expectations for the retail experience. We want to change that. We want them to enter our stores expecting to meet people who will care and help them. Our staff members are trained extensively so they have a high level of expertise. They are trained to sell what the customer needs, not what will pump up sales and profits in the short run. You only do the latter once with most people; they never come back if they feel they were pushed into purchases they didn't need.

We desire to build trust. That is supported by all our decisions involving our operational systems and how we train our team members. We take the long view. We strive to increase face time with our clients. Clients come before the task checklist, we tell our staff. If faced with a choice between the two, choose the clients. They deserve an exceptional experience.

In their book *The Discipline of Market Leaders*, Michael Treacy and Fred Wiersema reported on a major academic research project on successful companies. They found that they fit into one of three primary business models. They could be world class in one of them while only meeting market minimums in the other two.

One model is operations excellence, the Wal-Mart way of low prices and efficiency. Another is product innovation, think 3M, or BMW, or Mercedes, or Apple. Our story is about the pursuit of the third model, customer intimacy. We would provide the exceptional experience as well as solutions.

We realized that Pet Supplies Plus was not a national company in footprint. We had a decent size, but we could not be the price leader. And product innovation is tough for a retailer; we are the seller of other people's innovations. Therefore, we chose to put a stake in the ground and declare, "We are going to have the finest, most exceptional client experience that exists in the pet industry." What would differentiate us would be our people and how they dealt with our clients. We would innovate in how we sold to people at retail. People don't like to be sold to. Rather, they like to participate in the sale process, and that is what we do. We have also differentiated ourselves via our multistep, multimedia marketing system, which draws in new clients, nurtures our existing clients, and recovers lost clients systematically each month.

In your own business, your primary business model will determine how you structure your affairs, the kind of people you hire, the level of empowerment you give them, the systems you set up, and how you train. In the model of operations excellence, decision making is concentrated at the central office. The stores/offices/locations are expected to "follow the program," with minimum discretion. In the customer intimacy model, by contrast, the central office is kept small and lean. Its function is to support the locations staffed by highly talented and empowered employees.

For most entrepreneurs, the way to success is the customer intimacy model. It works best in differentiating the business. There just aren't that many Apples out there to lead in product innovation, and usually only one business can take the lead in operations excellence in any one category. It is tough for the average American entrepreneur to achieve the massive scale needed to become a price leader, and frankly it is not a lot of fun to do business that way either.

For the vast majority of small businesses, the best and surest way to success is to create an experience for the client or customer, whether you are a retailer, a local coffee shop owner, or a heating and air conditioning contractor. I know this from my experience in commercial banking and working with Main Street entrepreneurs for more than a decade.

As you turn these pages, you will find advice and tips that are based on my years of experience as an entrepreneur, my interaction with hundreds of successful entrepreneurs in my banking career, and the thousands of hours I have invested in learning through books, tapes, and seminars. I have taken some knocks and seen some successes. I believe that I have learned what works and what does not. I will be showing you business systems and what they involve. We will look at processes and personnel and the kind of customer relationships that assure a pleasant, productive, and repeatable experience.

Customer intimacy is our business model of choice. And we do not overdo it. We are not like that neighbor who is trying too hard to be friends. If clients want help, we provide it, but we do not make them feel it is forced on them. What we have done is develop a culture where people naturally reach out to others. It is an experience that you just cannot get in other stores. In your own business and industry, you too can learn to deliver that kind of experience.

It is not any one component of business that delivers it. Many components must work together, and in the ensuing chapters, we will examine each of them. Again, many types of businesses can apply these principles. They involve fundamentals of human nature.

What was I thinking and feeling that morning in 1996 when I drove off into new territory? I felt fear, for sure, but also an immense excitement. I was, after all, bucking all tradition on my own side of the family. You just did not leave a secure, high-paying job to chase a dream. My father worked thirty-two years at General Motors. My parents, who supported me incredibly well throughout my life, knew that what I was doing was risky, and they feared I would not be able to take care of my family.

But I had done the research, and I had gone through with it. I made the commitment to face my fears and never quit my quest for success. The only failure would be giving up completely. Win or lose, I knew my only real anguish would be regretting in twenty or thirty years why that young man never just took that chance.

I felt sad as I pulled down the road, the image of my family in the rearview mirror. But then I felt exhilarated. I drove six hours, around Chicago and up to Wisconsin, and when we arrived at our new home, I had more bounce to my step than at any time of my life. I had done it. I hadn't settled. I had been true to myself. I had an outlet for my passion, and I was thrilled that I took the leap of faith.

Chapter 1

POWER OF PASSION

You often hear of people setting out to make their fortune. Was it to make a fortune that I turned the ignition key in my packed van that day and headed for Wisconsin to launch a new career? Was it primarily the pursuit of riches that led me to head up that highway, uncertain of the turns?

I have done well financially, but my family and I have made a lot more than that. I can tell you with crystal clarity what motivated me. It was not so much a matter of what I was seeking, but rather, what I was following. I was following a passion.

Let me share with you a definition of passion that I think reflects the theme of this book and my own approach to business and leadership: Passion is when you put more energy, thought, and intensity into your pursuit than is required. It is about going the extra mile in everything you are passionate about. It is far more than simple enthusiasm or excitement. Passion is ambition and motivation that have developed into massive action. People of passion put as much of their heart, mind, body, and soul into something as they possibly can, and in the end they have nothing left. They threw their whole heart into the endeavor and have no regrets.

I believed that if I had stayed in my corporate career, I would have lost my passion and failed to reach my potential. Pursuing your passion is the key to finding and unlocking your potential. I was thirty-two when I left that career, and now all these years later, I can look back and see how my passion powered me through many difficult challenges. It was in the process that I discovered a gift for leadership and unlocked my potential in that area in a way that never could have occurred in my corporate career.

You might be thinking about something you really want to do. It could be a career change, applying for that job you think would be great inside your current company, or starting a business you have dreamed of. If you allow yourself to think of what could be and believe you can be successful, passion will begin to well up inside you and compel action.

Passion will drive you to a level of success and challenge that you would never have experienced. Passion will drive you to action. As I was losing passion late in my banking career, a lot of what I was doing felt like an obligation rather than being motivated to excel. Because I had lost my passion, I no longer felt that I couldn't wait to do my daily work.

Passion overcomes shortcomings in talent, resources, and brainpower. It propels you when others quit, and it galvanizes your team around you. Passion is caught rather than taught. If the leader is operating out of passion, others around him will rise to a higher level.

The Fuel of Accomplishment

My daughter, Lindsay, wants to have a career in elementary education, while my son has a passion to be a professional baseball player. Because they have a passion and a dream that moves them out of their comfort zone, both of them defer gratification to take on disciplines and activities that many kids their age won't. We always talk about doing things today that others won't, so that they have opportunities to do things others can't later in life. Passion is their fuel to become what they have set out to become.

I am a member of best-selling author Dr. John Maxwell's Maximum Impact Club. I have subscribed to his monthly materials for many years. I have read all his books that have been released into bookstores as well. Over the years I have learned many leadership lessons from him relating to passion. These include:

1. The difference between a good leader and a great leader is passion.

2. A passionate leader with few skills will outperform the passive leader with many skills.

3. Passionate leaders move an organization beyond problems into opportunities.

4. You can never lead something that you don't passionately care about.

5. You can never start a fire in your organization unless it is first burning in you.

6. Knowing information is valuable, but possessing the fire is invaluable.

If you are going to be an entrepreneur, then you have to become a leader. A person who lacks passion will lack the ability to effect positive change. One can only effect positive change through effective leadership of people. To lead people effectively, one must be an influencer of people. Passion is the key to being an influencer. Think about it. Who would you rather see each day at work, believe in, and follow: a passionless person going through the motions, or a person on a mission to build that cathedral?

I left my career with white-hot passion. I wanted to create a great company that would nurture and inspire others. I wanted to make a difference in the lives of individuals, other entrepreneurs, and the community. For my family, I wanted the freedom of time to enjoy experiences together and model a life of passion that would impact the thinking of my kids. That is what I set out to do that day, and I, along with great partners and a wonderful team, have done it.

With my Pet Supplies Plus franchise group, I wanted to create a client experience that had yet to be seen in the pet industry. It was never only about creating wealth. Wealth is better pursued indirectly. When you have a primary focus on wealth, it is harder to achieve. Instead, you want to focus on what leads to wealth. Figure out what drives it, and the wealth will come. That means adding value to others through products, services, and experiences. When this happens, revenues and profits will expand, leading to the creation of wealth.

I try to focus each day on just creating value in my business and making sure we have sound fundamentals in place in every area of the business, rather than waking up every day obsessively focused on a profit and loss statement and trying to financially engineer success. At the end of the day, every business has to drive revenue growth, and you cannot do that with a mindset of endless cost reductions. A cost containment philosophy coupled with strong revenue growth is a superior formula for long-term business success. An entrepreneur must invest in growth.

Making a Difference

A lot of people get into a business because it is a hobby or they are good at something specific, leading to a technician approach, and they struggle. I got into this business because I have a passion to create and innovate. I want to make a difference in people's lives. I love people, and I view myself as being in the people business. The beautiful thing for me is that my partners and key leaders feel the same way, so we have a culture of making a difference. I saw an opportunity to be a positive influence, to invest my life in something bigger than me, rather than just working in a job.

I knew that it would test me and challenge me beyond anything I could imagine and that I would have to continuously strive to learn and grow personally. I saw those as ways to enrich my life. They would energize me. I wanted to share that positive model with my children. The prospect of such healthy growth brought out in me the passion to succeed.

So many of the things we enjoy in life today are the result of some man or woman who had a passion and an idea. That is what made America great. The government helps to set up the playing field that allows the free expression of ideas, but we would have few players on that field were it not for the massive wealth creation of all the innovative products that this land of immigrants developed in the last few centuries.

Our human creativity makes us a vibrant society. Americans have long been celebrated for their entrepreneurial spirit, and you can attribute that to the richness of our cultural mix. America was founded by adventurous people who took the risk to leave their native land, and that was followed by waves of other immigrants. Entrepreneurialism is in our DNA.

I believe we are made in God's image, and since God is the ultimate creator, we are made to create too. This nation was founded on freedoms, including free expression. That is rare in this world. And that is what is exciting about the prospect for entrepreneurialism on these shores. Some of the talk from politicians is disheartening. They sometimes seem to demonize the entrepreneurs who built our system. Think of the consequences in *Atlas Shrugged*. We must not douse the flame of passion.

An Investment in Freedom

A business leader must find inspiration. I worked in corporate America for fourteen years, and it is a lifestyle that spins with the hands of the clock. You are tied to schedules and deadlines. You get too busy to dream. Risk taking and innovative thinking are much more difficult to practice and implement. Today, if I want to leave my office in the middle of the afternoon and find inspiration at Starbucks, I can do that. In fact, that is where I am this morning as I write this. If I have an idea that is innovative, I can get my team together, work on it with their input, and implement it. Implementing ideas and seeing them work is one of the great thrills of entrepreneurship. It feeds your passion.

Such freedom leads to better investment in the long run, and not just in business, but in family as well. I have missed few of my children's activities. Our family spends many hours together, taking frequent trips. Our family goal has been to see baseball games in all the major league parks across the country.

It is not that corporate workers are all unhappy in their roles and their jobs. Many work with dedication and find fulfillment. But as technology expands expectations about how quickly they must respond, they often find themselves more pressed for time than ever before. As one advances within an organization, one is also expected to commit more time. It may not be expressed directly, but it is communicated through the level of output that is required and the norms in the office, such as arrival and departure times from the office and Saturday office hours.

I do not correlate time with success. I try to be very strategic about what I do and how I build the business. An hour or two spent on developing the big picture, on deciding how and when to best go about doing things, may be far more productive than ten hours of busywork. Management of time for the entrepreneur is outside the scope of this book, but learning to be ruthless with time and who gets on the daily schedule and what to focus on each day is crucial to entrepreneurial success.

I was thinking strategically well before I got into the truck that day to leave for Wisconsin. I had a strategic vision for my family and our future and for what really mattered. I wanted my children to see that one must not settle but, instead, must recognize one's gifts and passions and pursue them diligently. I wanted them to see that one must not cave in to fears, avoiding all risks. So many people avoid danger and risk at almost any cost. That is no way to live. Becoming aware of one's gifts and weaknesses and investing time and resources in them leads to freedom. The freedom to make choices about your future comes from this investment and the belief in your own ability to be resourceful in any situation. One must invest in the things that lead to this kind of freedom of choice.

Heidi and I had a long time to think about such matters. We did not have children until we were thirty years old. By the time I had finished graduate school in my mid-twenties, I knew I wanted to be an entrepreneur. I started preparing. I knew that when we had children, I would want them to witness, by our example, that there was more to living than going to school, getting a job, and making money. Heidi and I wanted an approach rich in experiences and relationships. To be "rich" means to be far more than wealthy.

Taking the Plunge

By my early thirties, as the frustrations built in my banking career, the question was demanding an answer: "Am I going to do this, or not?" I had prepared myself. I had read extensively and pursued the right mindset. It was becoming increasingly difficult to be passionate about my corporate job. What put me over the edge was when someone in the top echelons put the brakes on that big media deal I'd worked on so hard. "This is just going to keep happening," I thought.

That is when my friend and I began talking about a Pet Supplies Plus franchise. I spent several months studying the industry. I'll never forget that Thanksgiving weekend of 1995 when my brother Dan and I traveled to Appleton and Green Bay, Wisconsin, and drove around. We drove up that Friday, and after seeing the community and where I would be setting up our first store, I called the franchise owner, not expecting that anybody would answer.

"I loved it!" I told Harvey Solway, then the executive vice president of franchising, when he picked up the phone.

"Well, it is yours," he said. "Plan on becoming a member of the team."

Within a few weeks, by Christmas, my wife and I made our final decision to go ahead with this adventure. I had more energy than I knew what to do with. I felt alive with excitement. That is so often how it works: Out of frustration is born something new and wonderful. A door closes; a door opens. Opportunities arise. When we look back at the parade of events in our lives, we often can see that our low points were simply when we began to rise to our high points.

BUILDING THE BRAND

I n his book *Pour Your Heart into It*, Howard Schultz of Starbucks tells of the inspiration he felt on a visit to Italy, when he observed how Italians would gather and enjoy conversation over espresso. It was the Italian cultural norm of the café being the center of social interaction and this sense of community that helped to inspire the Starbucks brand. It was Howard Schultz's passion that fueled his energy and persistence to build Starbucks into a global brand. His passion was more than just the desire to build a great company. Howard Schultz had a passion for the experience he wanted his customers to have that mirrored what he saw and experienced in Italy.

It takes passion to build a brand. Without it, you get into your daily routine, and any moments of inspiration will pass you by. It takes the passion of the leader to consistently communicate and teach the team to live the vision for the experience the brand represents. Vision alone is not enough: Passion propels you and sustains you to apply your force of will to the organization over an extended period of time to build the brand as a culture. When the odds seem insurmountable, you will forge ahead. You will never give up.

I see two major elements in building a brand: you have to be truly different, and you have to emotionally connect with the customer on some level. This is a very high standard or bar to achieve, but it is where you will find defensible, enduring niches that are highly profitable. Brands should stand for something that the buyer can count on and recognize as unique. And there needs to be an emotional appeal and connection.

Seth Godin, in his book *Purple Cow*, tells of an imaginary trip through France in which he admired the many fine brown cows—at first, that is. After a while, they did not seem so fine anymore; it was just one more brown cow after another. He imagined how remarkable it would be to see a bright purple cow, standing out vibrantly in the sea of brown cows. His point is that you have to approach your brand as if you are trying to create a purple cow.

Most businesses continuously make small, incremental changes that match what their competitors in the industry are doing. They seldom look outside their industry to learn from what other innovators are doing. In her book *Different*, Young Me Moon calls this "sliding into the sea of sameness." Eventually, everything you do is blah-blah-blah to the buyer.

Consumers are inundated with choices. What do retail consumers, or business-to-business buyers do when they have so many choices? They look at price. That is what ends up driving their decisions. There are apps for your smart phone that let you instantly compare retail prices. That kind of technology is going to proliferate in the next five years. In the B2B market, multiple proposals are the norm.

Unless you can create unique enduring value, something that makes you truly unique and differentiates you from the competition, you are dead. "Differentiate or die," says author Al Trout. What you want to do is change the buying criteria of your customers from price to something else. Our something else is solutions and expertise. We become our clients' trusted advisor for their everyday pet-care needs. Our clients know that we have their best interests at heart: we have changed their buying criteria from strictly price; we are their source for answers. That is a much better place to be in the mind of the buyer than the commoditized place of lowest price.

You want clients and customers to come to you for some other reason that is compelling and crystal clear and that cannot be missed or easily copied. You must find out what is truly valuable to them. This is extremely hard work. Entrepreneurs often get this wrong and wonder why the market doesn't embrace their vision.

Consider the surge of online shoppers. They are driven to compare prices. They can quickly assess features and find the cheapest price, often free of sales tax. But what are you missing when shopping is redefined as surfing and shipping? No longer do you touch the product before buying it , hold it, flip it over, perhaps try it on. No longer do you chat with the store employees about what might be best for you. You miss that whole sensory experience and the sales support. You might go into a store with your guard up, but if you feel comfortable and appreciated and get to know the people there, you will want to return. That is a reason that Starbucks became so successful: the coffee shops offered that sense of community to people increasingly hiding behind technology. They became that comfortable "third place" for those who don't want to be in the office but are not quite ready to head home.

The reality, however, is that anything that can be sold and serviced from a distance is at risk of being peddled on Amazon or by some other online seller. Strategically building a brand means creating something that cannot be entirely delivered by an online competitor. Personal expertise and relationships and experiences are hard to deliver online. Private label and proprietary products must be delivered locally by real people who engage with the customer. A sales process that is appreciated and valued by the end buyer cannot be commoditized on the Internet. The entrepreneur's task is to strategically think how to insulate his or her business from forces that would dilute its value.

People want community. They are starting to feel isolated, even amid the swirl of text messages and Facebook posts. I encourage my children to pick up the phone and talk to people rather than to fire off texts. Often they respond by looking at me as if I were from an alien planet, but they get the message. People need to communicate genuinely. It builds community, and we see that spirit in our stores as our clients come in, their dogs on a leash, and talk to one another and to the staff.

If a business doesn't create that sense of community and enduring value that is defensible, it can soon become commoditized, and when that happens the name of the game is merely price matching. A business that is being commoditized will look in every corner for cost reductions. Such a business cannot pay people appropriately, and so the employees do not give extra effort, which means they do not engage with the customer. Pressure mounts in every area of the business, impacting investment levels and vendor relations. Business ceases to be fun.

That is the state of banking today, and it is one of the biggest reasons I left that industry. It was frustrating to go the extra mile and be devalued; the customer would go with any lender offering a quarter-point-lower rate. That is not to say that banking cannot be delivered in a unique way. A commercial banker could create a group of clients who appreciate that banker's expertise and how he or she works through loan requests. I wasn't finding that to be the case, and my waning passion compelled me to change.

Any business can drive profit by relating to clients in a unique way. No matter what you are selling, you can build your sales force and your customer support in a way that is different from all the others. Is this easy? Absolutely not. I, along with key employees and my partners, have had to devote more than ten years of our best thinking and experimenting to land our company where it is today. But you have to start. You have to take risks and make mistakes. The journey is not along a straight path; it twists and turns, and you learn many lessons along the way.

You have to ask yourself, "How would I compete with myself? What are my competitors' weaknesses?" We surveyed our clients with questions such as, "What are your biggest frustrations and fears with being a pet owner?" and "What solutions have you tried and how is that working?" and "If you could fix these matters your way, what would you do?"

The surveys provided great feedback, and then we adjusted what we were doing. Most entrepreneurs think they know what people want and just open the doors and wonder why people do not come to them. It is harder, but it pays off, to ask the people what they want. That is how you get the information you need to build your brand.

Here are three big questions you can ask when establishing your brand:

1. What will our brand represent and be about?

2. What are the tangible ways that we will live out our brand each day?

3. How well do we know our ideal client, and what will we do to know them better?

The answers to these questions determine your messaging to the market, the people or businesses you target for your marketing efforts, and the type of people you employ. Training is driven off the answers to these questions as well. As you answer them, you can create systems and processes that will allow you to give the customer a repeatable experience.

Opportunities Abound

There are a multitude of franchise opportunities, or you can create your own business. It doesn't matter what business you choose, within reason. You might not want to try to sell buggy whips these days, but in most categories, if you can create a compelling offer, a unique selling proposition, and then follow the advice in this book, along with many other great resources available, you can succeed.

Before I chose to pursue Pet Supplies Plus, I looked at Subway and franchises in that category. I looked at printing services back in the early '90s but was concerned that the proliferation of desktop PCs was putting printing services at risk of being obsolete. I looked at the video business. I actually looked at some consulting-type programs in which you can buy a franchise and be a consultant to entrepreneurs. I passed on that because I hadn't yet been an entrepreneur. That doesn't stop some people.

I got into the pet industry because of my compelling desire to start in a business that could be different and that could connect emotionally with consumers, and therefore I could build a unique and successful brand. I saw the opportunity to make an emotional connection with our clients by becoming the trusted authority and advisor.

We felt that since people care for their pets as if they were their children, we could connect with them by positioning ourselves as having, in effect, a good bedside manner. That is why we offer nutrition expertise, with veterinarian school certification. That is the purpose of our training, not only in general pet care but also in positive psychology and consultative selling and leadership. All of this investment in our people has led to an amazing experience for our clients.

You will notice we call them *clients*. That is what we consider our customers to be. We aspire to gain their trust and treat them as far more than shoppers coming through the door. That is what made us different. That was our emotional connection. It was the path we took to create our brand. You can do that in any category. I just chose the pet category.

Examine the business you are in. Where is the opportunity to differentiate? Looking only at your competitors leads to that "sea of sameness." Look across industries to see what the innovators are doing. Can you innovate in how your customers are sold? Can whom you target and the focus of your business be what differentiates you? How about your follow-up after the sale? Can you be different in how your customer is treated from time of sale, and while he or she owns the product until buying again? Think about the three business models and ask yourself where you fit.

Appealing to Passion

Bad service annoys me, anywhere. My kids point out to me how often I remark on that, even on vacation. Businesses do such dumb things. Do they not realize what they are doing to themselves? It is hard to let it go. It is hard to relax when you see such flagrant violations of good practice.

In training with staff, though, it is essential that you not let these things go. You have to make sure that your staff is not alienating your client base. When you lose clients, not only have you lost their patronage, but they may steer away other potential clients. You need to stay on task with boundless energy. We use the term "constant gentle pressure" to describe our mindset in making sure we stay "on brand" all the time. It is this kind of vigilance toward creating the ideal experience that honors your brand vision. This is what drives successful companies, and it requires a passionate leader to pull off.

When you do these things right, people will see no acceptable alternative to you. They will drive right past your competitors because it is you with whom they have the relationship. They have bought into your brand with a passion because of your passion and the passion of your people

The brand of a business may strike us in various ways. There are brands that we merely tolerate yet continue to frequent. There are brands that we dislike. There are brands that we like a lot. And then there is the "passion brand," as author Kate Newlin called it in her book by that name.

A brand that appeals to a passion will strongly influence the actions of customers or clients. You stimulate their emotions, which imprints your brand more deeply upon them and leads to a stronger connection to your company. When you have a passion brand, you are competing in a different marketplace, with a different set of rules.

Recently I was traveling in a baseball tournament with my son, Collin. We got to South Bend, Indiana, and I had a lot of extra time between games, so I did a computer search and found out where all the Starbucks were in South Bend. I did not want to know about any other coffee shop. I wanted to know where the Starbucks were. I have been on numerous vacations and trips when I have driven two to three miles out of my way to find one. Starbucks developed its passion brand well. It is certainly one of mine.

Few businesses actually pursue passion brand status. They want to be logical and rational, and that is what produces average. Those who consider you a passion brand will wholeheartedly recommend you. They will accept no substitutes. They will go out of their way to get to you. They have a powerful relationship with your brand. They will also go out of their way to recommend your brand to friends, family, and colleagues. Passionate entrepreneurs put everything they have into creating a brand that produces passionate fans of the business, those "raving fans," as author Blanchard calls them.

In *The Passion Brand*, Newlin wrote about people whose decision on where to live in a city was based on a specific grocery delivery service. When it gets to the point where people are making decisions based upon your brand, she wrote, then you have a passion brand. I'm not sure it has to go that far to be a success, but I understand her point.

I am sure you can think of several passion brands. Ice cream, automobiles, jewelry, shoes—many industries have passion brands within them. There are businesses in your hometown that are not nationally known but locals rave about them. I am not suggesting that people will change where they live based on whether they are near a Pet Supplies Plus store, but we do want our clients to accept no substitute. Our goal is to become indispensable to our local community of pet owners.

In short, I want our clients to feel passionate about our business because it is business itself that is my own passion. I felt the calling to be an entrepreneur and to serve my clients, my employees, and my community. I do love pets, but I did not get into this business because I was a pet fanatic. Instead, I hire pet fanatics. I got into this business to pursue my passion to lead, to develop, and to have an impact and, yes, to create wealth along the way for me and my family to enjoy and give.

Is building a brand worth it? Yes. Is it easier to just run a tight business with a traditional approach and skip all this hard work? Sure, if you want what's average or enjoy the race to the bottom on price. Building a brand is worth it: Growth accelerates under a visionary brand idea that engages the human heart. It takes everyone in the organization on a journey that unlocks their passion and in turn their potential. Building a brand is most certainly difficult, but it is profitable, and it helps to secure your business from competitors, and it makes business fun.

Chapter 3

WHAT'S THE BIG IDEA?

In June 2008 our team acquired a five-store group of Pet Supplies Plus stores from a retiring owner within our franchise group in Birmingham and Tuscaloosa, Alabama. Only one of the five stores was performing at the time, so we acquired them at a good price.

As we were assessing the opportunity, we saw that the stores had a lot of good things going for them. They had good real estate and operations. They were clean and well run. They had quality people in key leadership roles. The average tenure of their managers was seven or eight years. But it was clear that the level of passion and engagement in their work and with clients was very low. There seemed to be no desire for being proactive and for growth. I did not have a clear understanding of what was needed at that time, but we went ahead with the purchase.

We made some changes, but I did not see those changes translate into sales growth. In fact, sales flatlined and then began to fall in the second year. Granted, it was a tough economy. But we do not use the economy as an excuse. We say that the only economy that matters to us is our one-on-one relationship with the client.

At that point, I made a key leadership change in our organization, and I stepped into a more direct, hands-on role with the markets.

It was really then, early in 2010, that I finally found my leadership point of view. I found my voice. That point of view was passion, and a strategic approach to growth and clients, would drive the business. From then on, my work each day within this acquired market as well as our other markets was to raise up a tide of momentum built on passion for serving our clients. We would strategically position our business around earning "trusted-advisor" status and build trust in everything we did. We would go the extra mile for our clients, and we would invest in expertise. The combination of expertise delivered by passionate employees going the extra mile would drive our success going forward.

I began to aggressively engage with our staff at all stores through-out the country that we own, sharing a vision for change with our team and inspiring them to reach higher and to reach out. What did we stand for? What were we really all about? Without a big idea to pursue, we would just be going through the motions. It was in that period that we worked on our big idea for our brand, in effect, answering that question of what we stood for.

We had research showing that a pet was good for your health. It was good for you physically, mentally, and emotionally. Studies show that having a pet will lower your blood pressure, improve your mood, and make you 40 percent more likely to exercise and to have other relationships. After all, many people have met while walking their dogs.

We decided that we wanted to improve the lives of our clients through positive pet ownership. That was our "big idea." That would be what would drive us. We also knew that owning a pet can feel overwhelming at times. We chose to become our clients' advocates so that they could tap in to the benefits shown in the studies. We wanted to make having a pet a much more positive and easier experience.

An Amazing Formula

We came up with a three-tiered approach. After we stated our big idea, which, like a cathedral, is something bigger than ourselves, we drafted our purpose statement: We want to make the day of our clients and their pets better. Our purpose is what guides our behaviors. A cashier might have had a bad day, but when she comes into the store, she remembers that she needs to attend to the purpose. And third, we drafted our mission statement: We would become the trusted advisor to one client per day per store who would enthusiastically refer Pet Supplies Plus to friends and family. The mission statement really is our business strategy.

We put all that in place, along with an approach to hiring that will be covered in a later chapter, and what happened was amazing. I saw much higher levels of engagement in the stores. People became excited about what they were doing. They saw something to shoot for. Those five stores alone have grown 30 percent in the last two years. That would be a little more than double the pace at which the average pet specialty retail store would have grown during that time period. The good news is that this stuff works.

We included our mission statement in our e-mails, under our signature block. I have an internal blog that I write weekly. For about a year, I wrote posts about our mission statement and how it ties in to our business strategy and our position relative to our competitors.

In our business, clients want access to expertise. The vet is the supreme expert, but access is difficult. You have to schedule an appointment and pay a lot of money. The typical pet store has easy access but a low level of expertise. We have invested much time and money over the last decade in building expertise, but what really kindled the inner passion of our employees was our effort to build our big idea and purpose and mission. That is how we have become

the trusted authority in pet care for our clients. We are not veteri-
narians, of course, but our people can handle many of pet owners'
everyday issues. In that way, we offer greater accessibility than a vet,
and we provide the expertise that our competitors do not offer.

Besides my blogging, I spent a couple of years traveling extensively and spending a lot of face time talking to our staff about why
this matters and helping every employee understand his or her role
as it relates to the mission statement. One of my partners now is personally coaching each of our store managers on living out the mission
statement and our playbook. He goes around several times a year to
have a one-on-one session with each manager.

Any entrepreneur should be able to see the importance of having
a big brand idea. You need to have a purpose, and you need to have a
mission, and you need to understand how you can improve the life of
your customer. When you develop your mission statement, you are
stating your strategy for providing unique value to the market. You
are signaling what makes you different.

In that way, you can inspire your employees. Gen Y, the generation born in the 1990s and later, is similar to the World War II generation in that they are civic-oriented and altruistic. Their mindset
is completely different from that of the baby boomers and Gen X.
Those generations are more individualistic. Many of them focused
on themselves, their careers, their investments. Members of the new
generation tend to be different. They have a sensitive "BS" meter.
They do not like people or organizations that lack authenticity. They
want to pursue something bigger than themselves.

Employers have observed that trend, and I can corroborate that
through my observations of how my own employees act. I have read
research that has identified a cycle that swings back and forth between
an individualistic society and a civic society. And because the latter

is the mindset of the newest generation, that is the way you have to engage them. Authenticity and credibility are supreme in the minds of today's customer. Be sure your message is on trend with this cycle.

In addition, you have to ask your customers what's important to them, what their fears and frustrations are with products or services, and then adjust what you are doing to meet those concerns. That takes work, but here's the payoff: your employees gain a lot of confidence that you have a winning business strategy, and they get excited because you engage them in the process.

This is not something I just dreamed up one day. I got our employees involved in it, and they believe in it. Any business owner can do the same thing we have done and get the same results, regardless of the industry. We try to use a lot of different venues to communicate it, and I am still trying to think of more.

Understanding Your People

In short, entrepreneurs need to stay attuned with how their customers and clients see things, and they have to understand the mindset of their employees as well.

TOMS Shoes, for example, makes footwear based on a style long worn by Argentinean farmers, and for every pair the company sells, its nonprofit affiliate donates a pair to children in need. The company has tapped into a constituency that is motivated to buy from it because the purchase does something good for somebody else. It has tapped into a sense of altruism that drives purchase. The company's employee base must likewise feel passionate about going to work every day, whether in accounting or marketing or running the servers, because every sale means some kid in a village gets shoes.

That is the kind of relationship between a business and its employees and customers that drives success. They are in alliance, sharing a sense of loyalty and purpose.

Jim Stengel, author of the book *Grow*, is a former marketing manager for Procter & Gamble. He did a major study that he calls the Stengel 50 Growth Index and concluded that the fifty greatest brands in the world share one trait: They are oriented around improving the lives of their customers through their use of, and interaction with, the brand. Every one of them has a compelling statement on how they are going to do so.

If you have such a goal, it should drive every decision in your business. Our goal is to improve the lives of our clients through positive pet ownership, so that informs how we treat them in our stores. It informs our training programs, policies, and our marketing message.

In recent years, we have further defined our relationship with those who patronize our stores by referring to them as "clients" instead of "customers." When you think "customer," you think of a transactional relationship based on price and convenience. The consumers view you as a commodity. "There is really no difference," they say, "so I'll buy from whoever is the cheapest." That is death for a business. I concluded that how people refer to us is partly a reflection of how we refer to them. Changing the language to "client" helped to advance our mission and purpose and vision.

The word *clients* communicates the role we desire: that of the trusted advisor. A client is what lawyers have, and accountants, and other professionals. Clients expect that the professional has their best interests at heart. When a business adopts that expectation, the consumer's buying criteria changes from pricing and convenience to something more valuable: an expectation of expertise and trust. We want our clients to believe that when they go into one of our stores, they will get trustworthy advice that is in their best interest, not just for the benefit of our business.

Using the word *clients* also helps to activate our employees' passion to serve. It is not enough for the entrepreneur to have only passion. You have to awaken that passion in your people. And what I have learned is that the best way to do that is to give them a vision bigger than themselves, one that they can embrace. It also requires that they be a part of the creation of that vision because then they own it and are intrinsically motivated to live it out.

Far More than Numbers

One of the things I have learned was that when I focused strictly on the numbers, I could improve things incrementally, but eventually a strictly numbers orientation chokes the life out of an organization. Revenues flatline because there is no engagement by the team. Risks are no longer taken that catapult a business to a new level of growth. It is important, of course, to know the numbers and have accountability in place. But an obsession with strictly the numbers will be to the detriment of execution and growth.

When you turn that around, the revenues begin to accelerate. For us, that has meant growth rates that were double for our industry. We are projecting earnings nearly ten times higher than they were just two years ago. We had double-digit growth rates, but our earnings are growing nearly tenfold.

Two big lessons came out of this for me: 1) CEOs and owners must personally create and reinforce vision and purpose, and 2) when they do so, it pays off on the bottom line. This is a task you cannot delegate. Investing in such "soft" business aspects as leadership development, relationships, and mission will result in excellent growth in revenue and profit.

Let's look at the first lesson: the need to continually reinforce vision. The entrepreneur must actively engage in this critical function with a lot of passion. Vision can leak away like air out of an old tire. You must not let your company go flat. That is what happens to a vision if the leader doesn't continually communicate it to the team.

The sense of excitement always has to come from the top down. It is how it works with a great sports team: you always find an inspirational, motivational coach. I was a basketball coach for five years. I am a fan of Michigan State's college basketball team.

Their coach, Tom Izzo, is probably one of the top five coaches in all of college basketball in America. Anyone who watches him at work knows he is the walking embodiment of passion. But when the school hired him, people were disappointed and unsure. He had been a little-known assistant coach, and they were hoping for a name coach. But Izzo has been to the Final Four several times since 1996, and the Michigan State basketball program is ranked in the top twenty every year. They have been to fifteen consecutive NCAA tournaments. Through passion and, I am sure, good strategy, Coach Izzo has demonstrated that an unknown leader with a clear sense of mission can build a winning program or business.

Every aspect of Coach Izzo's leadership of the Michigan State program is about passion. You can see it on the sidelines. I think he works as physically hard as his players do. You can see his animation when they make a great play. You see him run from the corner baseline all the way to half-court with his players, urging them on. At the end of a game, he's sweaty and hoarse.

The players, the people on the team—whether it is a sports team or your business team—will take note of that spirit. It infuses the whole organization. I tell store managers to envision themselves as a coach. They set the pace and the tone for their store and think strategically about the team and how to motivate it. Either you or the leaders you have in place must live with this kind of passion if you want to enjoy extraordinary results.

The second lesson comes down to this: Such enthusiasm emanating from the top will do wonders for your bottom line. That is because your clients respond to the passion. They trust you and patronize you. They stay longer with you. Others take note of their loyalty and come to see what it is all about. You retain more people, you attract more, and that is when revenues and profits blossom. Referrals accelerate growth. It is a self-fulfilling cycle.

All of this adds up to a strong, successful business that has the ability to make a difference, not only in the lives of clients and employees but also in the community. And by making Main Street stronger, you make America stronger.

Most businesses find themselves on a treadmill, constantly losing and gaining customers or clients. The trick is to slow that way down. We use the metaphor of a bucket with a hole in the bottom. You can fill the bucket with water and carry it around for a while, but you soon have to return to the pump, and that is a lot of walking. It will wear you out. Better to mend that hole. It may still leak a little, but look at how much faster the bucket fills and how much less water you waste. You can stay on task. So creating this kind of culture in your organization accelerates growth through more positive word of mouth, resulting in referrals and higher loyalty among your existing clients. When client acquisition and retention improve, rapid growth results. The bucket fills and stays full.

"Cloudy in the Pulpit, Dark in the Pews"

How do you make this come to life? Again, you must gain complete buy-in from your employees on your big idea, purpose, and mission. They must participate in shaping and creating those aspects of your business. They must get the message in many ways. So communicate your vision in a multimedia way. Take advantage of e-mail, blogs, personal visits, and continuing training. We commissioned an artistic rendition of our brand idea in the form of a waterfall. We call it our brand mural.

So that there is no ambiguity, define what living the vision looks like for each role in the company. There is an old saying: "If it is cloudy in the pulpit, it is dark in the pews." If the leader is not clear in his or her own head and cannot communicate clearly, the team will not have a clue how to live the mission and pass it on.

Share stories about people who succeed. We have a "Wins" column on our internal website where people can post examples of how they have lived the mission and it worked out great for the client. In our Appleton, Wisconsin, store, our staff had a longtime client who had to put her dog down. The client was distraught. Our team did something that seems small: everyone signed a condolence card, and they mailed it to the client. She came in, very touched, and a few weeks later returned with a new puppy and told the team that because of their thoughtfulness, she'd never think twice about where to take her business. How many other people do you suppose she told how she was treated? Such gestures send waves throughout the community and bring people to your door.

It is all about people, really, and your employees are central to the formula for success. We have distilled our core beliefs about people: They all are highly valuable and worthy of investment. The relationships between employee and employer must be mutually beneficial, not merely transactional. You need to get involved in their lives and make a difference. Do more than just pay them and expect them to do things. We set the bar higher. Whether they will stay with our company or not, we invest in them, celebrate them, help them pursue their dreams.

After all, the team, those who face the client each day, are the real test of whether you have a brand or not. They deliver the brand to the client. So many large companies invest millions of dollars in branding-oriented marketing, and then invest next to nothing in the front-line people who define daily what the brand really is for the client. The effect is that clients see one version in the magazine, television, and radio ads and another when they interact with employees.

We communicate that message to our staff all the time, particularly to our young employees. The message is this: "We realize that this may not be where you will work your whole career, but you can learn a whole lot here that will help you be successful. So share with us what it is you want to do and how we can help you to get there." When you communicate that, you have a far more engaged employee, whether he or she is with you one year or several. Your people know you care about them.

In business, the approach with people must be to deal with them with absolute integrity. You want to be more than technically right; you want to be above reproach. A business must serve people and have a positive influence and impact on them and the communities in which it operates. A business is an extension of who the entrepreneur is and aspires to be.

In short, those are our core beliefs about people. When a leader adopts that kind of mindset and communicates it effectively, people are going to go the extra mile for you. They are going to give you the discretionary part of their heart, and business is all about creating an experience for the client. Whether you are dealing in retail sales of carpeting or furniture or selling products to other businesses, you must create an experience that people enjoy and trust. How well you do so will become your defining characteristic.

Computers do not deliver experiences. People do. The only way you are going to consistently succeed is to develop a company culture in which your people strive to deliver that experience for the client. And to do that, a leader must connect with employees at a heart level. It is simply good for business.

A Mission, Not a Mishmash

And what of those who mock the mere mention of a mission statement as highfalutin and meaningless language? You counteract that by making sure that is not what you are producing. Sometimes a mission statement is created by a committee that wants it to be all things to all people, and the result is a generic mishmash that means nothing to anyone.

I resisted having a mission statement for nearly fifteen years. Finally, I realized that it could be simple. Ours is very tight. It says, "We want to be the trusted advisor." It is specific, and it establishes a goal toward which we can take meaningful action. Based on that, we strive to earn the trust of somebody every single day in every store, so that person will enthusiastically tell others about us.

The key is to be focused, to make the statement concise, narrow, and meaningful. We did not say, "We want to be the trusted advisor, have the lowest prices, offer the highest quality products, and provide the best service." You can see how that would make some employees gag.

Again, the message must come from the top down. It is the leader's job to drive communication around the vision. The entrepreneur must establish that specific vision with clarity and focus so that it comes across loud and clear all the way down to the employees who stock the shelves. It is certainly a plus if you can involve groups of employees in the formation of the vision as we did, but ultimately it is the role of the leader to do this. It is my job to communicate that message. I do engage our key leaders, but I do not let the message get diluted. Part of my job is to ensure consistency among our leadership, but at the end of the day, I am the one who makes the call. I maintain control over the message.

These thoughts on the role of the entrepreneur apply also to leaders within an organization. Those leaders are responsible for ensuring that the vision of the company is transferred from an owner or CEO to the employees who define the brand each day for the clients.

A Cultured Attitude

We had an employee with a serious illness who needed months of time off. I talked to my partners, and we decided that we would pay him during those months so that he could recover properly. We did not have to do that, but we have a long-term investment in him and in his leadership. It would be shortsighted to consider only a store's annual profit. We looked past that and said, "This is the right thing to do for this employee with a young family." In the years ahead, that investment comes back with untold dividends. It engenders goodwill in the workforce, and goodwill tends to spread to clients, who begin coming to our stores.

When I was telling one of our company leaders about my family's goal to get to every major league ballpark across the nation, he told me how much he'd like to get back to Fenway Park in Boston just one more time with his father. He explained that his father was dying. I mentioned this to others, and the company rallied to the cause. Several people got involved, including one of our investors, who obtained Red Sox tickets. We worked it out with our employee's wife so that it was a surprise, and we arranged the airfare, hotel, rental car, and admissions. "Here," we told him, "you are going to meet your dad and have a great time in Boston." His father was able to see his favorite team again before he died a year or two later.

I was proud of our company and how so many people reached out to this man. He's a key leader and a driver of our company's culture, and certainly, what the company demonstrated to him was that it has a culture with heart.

Your company's culture trumps all else. Culture even trumps strategy. If it is not right, nothing else matters. It translates into interactions with clients and their experience with your brand, and it thereby creates value. It is that simple.

It should go without saying that your culture must be ethical and trustworthy. If you do not have that reputation, you are done. It is your entry ticket into the game, so do not even think about getting in without it. And you can blow it quickly. It takes years to build your reputation, but you can destroy it in a moment. That is something we all should know by the time we are a young adult.

You must do things right in every direction, and that means not only with clients but also with your employees and with vendors and with the government, as in paying taxes. My partners and I want to sleep well at night. If we cannot operate this business the right way, then we need to sell it. If we are in the game, we are going to play by the rules.

When I say "by the rules," I mean following the rules of fair treatment and ethical behavior. I do not mean following typical business approaches that I have concluded do not work. Carrot-and-stick leadership is something of the past generation. I grew up with it. I tried it in my own company. It doesn't work anymore. Later in this book, I will share with you some other incentives that I do find quite effective.

For the most part, money incentives have never worked. The pay must be appropriate for the job, but beyond that, it ceases to be a big motivator. What we have found is consistent with what research has established: people want to work in a great environment where they feel appreciated, and for a company that they feel invests in them. Within a great culture, as described earlier, money can be a part of the overall incentive package to drive forward with great business results. So, the point is not that money never motivates, but in a bad culture, it fails to sustain motivation. The best people simply look elsewhere until they find the whole package.

Do you give your people training and coaching that inspires and motivates? That is a good start. You need to demonstrate the kind of leadership that makes people voluntarily follow you. No amount of external motivation will work if the motivation is not coming from within. You want employees who pursue the vision and serve the client simply because that is what they want to do. That is what makes the mission possible.

Daniel Pink in his book *Drive* outlines three major elements of a culture that will produce intrinsically motivated employees who engage. Those elements are 1) autonomy, 2) a path to mastery, and 3) purpose. In our organization we have built into our strategy, job design, and training the components to bring those drivers of motivation into play each day with excellent results. As you evaluate your culture, ask yourself if you can identify those three drivers in how you operate your company.

Chapter 4

DEVELOPING BRAND AMBASSADORS

I want to tell you about Holly, Amy, and Sarah.

Holly was a part-time cashier in our very first store during the first couple of years that we were in business. She wasn't focused on management but instead had other career interests. She had a long-term dream: to work in the medical field as a nurse.

During the time she was with us, we taught her things about excellence, having a good mindset for success, being reliable, and having good people skills. Holly already had those skills, and we helped her refine them.

When she left us, she went to work for Midwest Airlines. We have stayed in touch with her for sixteen years. Eventually she went to school to pursue her dream of becoming a nurse, working two jobs while she went to night classes.

Holly recently graduated with her four-year nursing degree. She took the long road. She did not have any help financially, so she had to work and save up money and get through. Now, she's pursuing her next level of goals. We are really proud of her, and I talk to Holly to this day.

Amy, who worked for us not long after we opened, was an outgoing and talkative young woman with great people skills, but at first, she had trouble with focus. Sometimes she'd wander from the cash register and would be chatting with clients rather than helping people check out. Good instinct, bad timing. We had to work with her on that, and over time, with training and attention, she excelled.

Amy graduated from high school and went to college, and she's now a project manager at Harley-Davidson in Milwaukee. A project manager must be detail-oriented and focused. I remember this kid, at sixteen years old, who was none of that, and I am proud of her, and of the small role we could play in her development.

Sarah started with our company in the late '90s. She started as a part-time cashier and was conscientious and eager to learn. Over time, she demonstrated a good work ethic and attitude, so we put her through our leadership program and life-skills development program. Soon she was starting to handle supervision shifts. We would move her out of her cashier role occasionally.

Then she told us she wanted to move to Minneapolis to attend college. There was a franchisee of our company in Minneapolis, so she applied there when she moved. We gave her a good reference. Now she's in a key leadership role with that group of stores.

Helping People Is What We Do

Young people often come to us with great potential and innate abilities but in need of training and development to bring out their best. In a sense, the company is functioning as a mentor. We size up employees' strengths and weaknesses and make the best of their strengths and help them overcome their weaknesses. We partner with them to help them become the best employees, the best people they can possibly be. It is a partnership, however. If the employee doesn't want to grow and improve, then nothing will happen. Our attitude is whether they continue with us or go off for their education and a different career, we are happy to be part of their lives. Helping people is what we do.

Now and then, we must tell an employee that he or she is simply not a good fit for us, and that too helps them. People whom we have helped transition out of the company have sometimes come back to thank us. Where they landed has worked out far better for them. They are grateful for our honesty because it led them to soul-searching and learning what they were truly more wired to do.

On a fundamental level, you have to value human beings. That is our approach. It all fits together. Your brand cannot profess to offer an intensely human experience if you do not take that approach yourself inside the company. Some companies try to declare, just by fiat, that they have great service. It doesn't work that way. You have to engage and invest in people to gain the discretionary part of their heart.

Holly, Amy, and Sarah are just three among many such success stories I could relate. Our former employees always are welcome to come back and talk to me, or anybody else in our company, and see how we can help them. We invest a lot of time, energy, and money in our staff, and that is the measure of our dedication. We want a work force that is engaged and competent. As I have pointed out, the best way I have found to differentiate oneself in business is to solve a client's problem and deliver a unique experience. The only way you can deliver that kind of experience that is truly unique is to do it through people.

And those people—your staff—cannot do that unless they are passionate, excited, trained, and dedicated to serving your clients or customers. Unless your people are interested and involved, what you are left with at the end of the day are numbers on paper. You are ignoring what's truly going to attract business. Your big idea, your brand, must excite and capture the hearts of people. It has to engage human emotion.

That is why, from the moment new employees come into our company, we focus on developing them.

Developing Relationships

A core element of our people strategy is relationships. Every leader in our company studies Dr. Maxwell's book *Developing the Leader within You*. One of his major concepts is called the five levels of leadership, and that is the core of our leadership development program. It starts with relationships. We have to have a great relationship with our own people if we want to have great relationships with our clients. They go together.

It was through Doug Bennett, the friend who, with wife, Sherry, spent the eve of our move to Wisconsin with us, that I learned about Dr. Maxwell. I had been a reader and a learner, but I hadn't been a student of leadership, and I realized I needed to become one if I was going to achieve the goals I had for myself and my family.

Developing the Leader within You is the best book I have ever read on leadership in how it communicates a difficult, complex subject in a simple way. We use Dr. Maxwell's definition of leadership extensively in our company. "Leadership," he says, "is influence, nothing more, nothing less." The ability to influence people is based on where the leader stands with each individual.

When a person is first appointed into a leadership role, he or she is a "positional leader" only, meaning people only follow because of the title. They follow the positional leader because they have to do so.

What we teach our leaders is to find common ground with every employee. Build a relationship with them. It doesn't mean they have to be best friends or do things socially outside the company, but it is important to find ways to make connections with them. Dr. Maxwell calls this advancing from positional leadership to "permission" leadership. People now follow because they want to, and they know that the leader cares about them. This is moving from level one to the second level of leadership.

The next level of leadership requires the leader to demonstrate excellence. The leader needs to be results oriented and demand that of the team. This is the "production" level. People then follow the level-three leader not only because they know that this person cares and that they have a relationship but also because they respect the leader's work and see how it helps the company.

The fourth level of leadership is "reproduction," which means the leader has built relationships, demonstrated competency, demanded it of the team, inspired the team to action, and now has a strategic focus on reproducing leaders. In other words, he or she is teaching leadership to associates, who then feel empowered to try things and learn on their own.

At the fourth level of leadership, people follow for an additional reason: They know what that leader has done for them. They see the investment, and they are grateful. This is when an organization experiences explosive growth and tremendous synergy within the team. Trust is at a high level, so initiatives are implemented quickly. The natural result is growth.

This progression in leadership can take a year or more. I teach my leaders that they are at a different level with each employee; they need to know where they stand with each, and have a plan to move to the fourth level. This type of thinking and action is a core activity of our company. Building leaders results in building brand ambassadors, who in turn deliver a great experience to the client.

Dr. Maxwell also includes a fifth level of leadership, one that few people achieve. Those who reach the fifth level have practiced good leadership for decades. It has become part of who they are and how they are known. I have been in business sixteen years, and I do not think I have achieved that level. By the end of my business career, I would hope that people will say that I reached it. It is a noble goal, but for now, we focus on the first four levels with our people.

Our entire philosophy about people is a process of starting from the ground and cultivating employees so that they deeply appreciate all we have done for them. We become known as an organization with a penchant for doing that, and we hope people seek us out because of that. In all of our stores, this process goes on every day. When we multiply that across an entire organization, a healthy environment is created in which people can excel. This leads to a team that is intrinsically motivated. In other words, they are excited and passionate about their day, and they do not need any outside push to work harder or more creatively. They appreciate us and show gratitude. They put their heart into their work, and that is the core of our people development process. It is the core of our brand.

Atmosphere of Encouragement

Encouragement is essential. I believe that my job as the leader of our company is to keep the flames burning brightly and to eliminate anything and everyone who tries to dampen those flames. Dr. Maxwell talks about "fire lighters" and "fire fighters." We do not want to douse an employee's flames; we want to fan them. Fire fighters are not welcome in our company.

In as many ways as I can, I try to encourage people and keep the vision out in front of them. My store leaders need to think like the best of coaches, who cultivate hearts and minds. They build relationships and trust. At their core, excellent coaches have the gift of encouragement. They have passion and lead with it.

Sometimes a coach invests a lot of time and effort into a player just to see that player join another team. Yes, that is a risk, but it is not a reason to give up trying. Out of ten people you develop, you might lose three or four, but the other six or seven help you build a dynamic organization. If you do not try just because you might lose someone, you are hurting yourself. You are giving in to cynicism. It is no way to live. Should you never love anybody because there is a chance you might get hurt?

People often ask me how we can run a business that is so spread out—we have stores in Michigan, Alabama, Texas, and Wisconsin—and manage to make it successful. After all, none except the Michigan stores are a quick drive from where any of us on the leadership team live, and the flights are complicated because we do not live in a hub city.

Here is the key: The executive leaders are not doing everything. We have leaders distributed all over this company who love what they do. They feel empowered, trusted, encouraged, and they do not do anything counterproductive to our goals. We have had occasional problems, but I do not have to be the one to catch them. My own people put a stop to it because they do not want the culture and future of the company compromised.

Our Hiring and Training System

Before we hire anyone, he or she has to go through a work-style test that is a profiling tool to help us gauge fit. We use this heavily and combine it with the application and interview to make the final decision. There has to be a strong overriding reason for someone to be hired who is not on profile. The payoff for our business is that we are assured everyone in the organization is a relatively good-to-excellent fit with the type of work involved, which makes leading much easier. As a result, the buy-in to our vision is high because people who would fit in poorly do not become part of the picture. The profiling test, then, is the first step of our hiring process.

In addition, we have an excellent software system for the onboarding of new hires. It makes the new employee's introduction to our company go smoothly. In the first sixty days, the employee's experience is highly scripted. That communicates clearly that we are on top of our game and know what we are doing. It gives the new hire a good impression of our company and makes him or her feel valued. If you have ever been hired by an organization and got stuck at a desk and left alone, wondering what you were supposed to do, then you know the feeling. We avoid that. It is an area in which we have worked hard, and we continue striving to improve the experience of each new employee.

The training is pretty much set for the first year. Each employee is required to work through a nine-module online education in pet care. As the employee completes a certain amount of training, a pay raise is given. Typically, employees can increase their pay 20 percent or more with these modules, which are to be completed within the first year. The store managers each have a private coach who works with them on the overall building and growing of their stores. This training includes outside marketing consulting, training in consultative sales, and general entrepreneurial training. The goal is to teach the store managers to view his or her role as that of a small-business owner.

We also use Lee Milteer's monthly *Millionaire Smarts* coaching program, which includes written materials, an audio CD of a guest-expert interview, and a transcript. It is all on positive mindset and success thinking. The Milteer materials are a recent addition to our training system. The one area that I was finding that was lacking in our people was a consistent positive psychology. I was trying to teach it and work on it myself. I have applied it in my own life.

In the last few years, I have realized I cannot do everything myself anymore, so more and more I am going out and finding experts whom I can bring into our business to give us the boost we need. That is the focus of Milteer's program, and the format enables me to distribute it widely. About sixty people a month in our company are getting this training. There is no way I can meet with sixty people a month who live in four states.

Another piece of our training system—and it is a major one—is our thirty-day action plan. One of our people in Alabama came up with this idea, which has enhanced the consistency of our training. Under the thirty-day action plan, each store manager meets with every single employee in his or her store once a month to do an informal evaluation. They discuss strengths and weaknesses and gaps in training. They pick one or two things that the employee will focus on for the next thirty days. At the end of the month, they discuss how the employee performed and talk about the next month. When I go to the stores, I can review the files that the manager keeps for the action plans.

There are no surprises. The employees know exactly where they stand. The manager doesn't build up unexpressed frustrations with the employees. The thirty-day action plans eliminate the dynamics that cause problems in employer-employee relationships.

At the same time, crucial, difficult conversations are happening. One problem of leadership is that people may avoid the pain of a tough conversation. We teach our people that it only gets worse if you avoid it. You need to identify the issue and deal with it on a regular basis. The employee will respond to that much better than if you hold off. A lack of communication always makes matters worse. You can apply that to relationships between husband and wife, parent and child, and to friendships. This is a matter of basic human decency and responsible relationships. You need to build trust.

In our company, training is done by job function. Each job, of course, has its own path. Leadership training is for all supervisors and future supervisors, those whom we have identified as having that potential. Every employee, however, must go through the pet-care training, and store management personnel also go through a nutrition certification by an animal-nutrition professor at Michigan State University, Dr. Sarah Abood. This means each store has three or four certified pet nutritionists to advise clients.

Our hourly employees get pay raises tied to completing the pet-care modules. Their progress is a good indicator of motivation and fit. If we find that someone is not doing well in this area, it suggests clearly to us that he or she is not very motivated and is not interested in the material. We start making alternative plans for that individual.

We also do training in what we call the rail, the five key touch points that every client will experience upon coming into our stores. We call it that because I want everybody on the rail at all times. I do not want them jumping to the right or left. I want consistency. It simply means that all clients who walk in the door will be greeted, and then an employee will engage them in the aisle. After they have settled on their purchase, we ask them if they have their loyalty card, or we give them the opportunity to get one, since the card includes so many benefits. We thank them and offer to carry out the heavy purchases of elderly clients and women. That is the "rail." It is the basic experience we want every client to have every time in our stores. We determined that if we could execute without fail this simple set of expectations, we would stand out in the retail landscape. I'll explain more about these touch points in the next chapter.

Our employees also are trained in what we call our playbook. The six elements of our playbook are the key drivers of success for our stores. If the store manager focuses his entire team on pursuing these six elements, the store will be successful. It is meant to be a simplified communication device to help them set priorities. Each store leader is expected to focus on the playbook's directives. There should be no ambiguity on expectations, so the playbook gives us alignment throughout the organization around a fixed set of objectives.

Here are the aims of our playbook, which constitutes the core of our training:

- To live and teach our mission and purpose daily
- To develop and foster alliance partnerships
- To engage in personal networking outside the store
- To make client retention calls
- To set thirty-day goal plans for the store
- To set the thirty-day action plans for employee development

The key idea here is that our organization has defined the key elements that drive our business. Any business can develop its own playbook. This set of drivers helps to answer the question, "What shall we focus on today and in the future?" Rather than doing hundreds of things with average effectiveness, we focus on these vital few and execute them with excellence.

Communication at the Core

Communication is central to success, and our company and I do our best to make sure our goals and philosophy stay foremost in the minds not only of our leadership but also of every employee in every store. Good communication, we have found, fosters good morale and enthusiasm. The old saying is true: "What people are not up on, they are down on."

We have a conference call every week with the regional managers of our four regions as well as with the executive team in our home office. Additionally, I write a weekly CEO blog, an internal communication that continually reinforces important themes. As this book is being published, we are beginning an internal employee newsletter that communicates the same themes as in the blog, as well as features on employees, training in mindset, and other important communications.

Our brand idea, playbook, and the rail are all communication devices that we use to promote alignment throughout the organization. Vision leaks, and without continuous communication to reinforce what is most important, the organization can begin to lose its way. On the other hand, a well-executed communication plan can galvanize employees to perform at a high level and bring that extra energy needed to wow our clients each day.

Every month, those thirty-day action plans for each employee go far in advancing communication and clarity. In our stores we also coach managers using well-developed visual aids that teach our playbook, brand idea, and the rail.

In addition, when the sales are reported each week, our regional managers do a summary write-up of results for their region, and they add a commentary on the results for their stores. We have found that the managers really love the feedback. Every week they wait to find out what the regional managers have to say about their store and how it has performed. The regional managers choose one or two areas weekly and encourage better results. I keep tabs on what the regional managers say. That is a gauge for me to know that the big ideas of our brand and priorities are filtering down from me to them to our front-line people.

I also do thank-you notes. I try to write two or three a month to various people on stationery that carries our brand. I'll send out the occasional e-mail when a store hits a new threshold and congratulate the team. Sometimes when a store is having a little rough patch, I'll try to encourage the staff to just stay focused on the playbook and not to worry about what it does not control.

I try to be in our markets quarterly, visiting all the stores. On a typical visit, I will line up meetings all day long, forty-five minutes at a time. I sit and listen to the people who are managing personnel. I ask questions. We talk about personal, financial, and professional goals. I want them to know that they have been heard, and by listening, I learn a lot about the company and what's going on, not only in the pet business but with our people.

Earlier in our company's history, I traveled to the markets more often. As we have grown in scale, I have empowered our regional managers to provide more of the leadership in the areas of store operations and culture development at the store level. I recognized that, as our company grew, I needed to change my role to remain in a strategic mindset.

Cultivating Loyalty

Cultivating loyalty starts with the leader's actions. If you treat people well, the way you'd want to be treated, that is a great start. You have to invest in their development. When employees feel as if they are just a number and that their relationship with the company is purely transactional—as in "you give me money, I give you work"—it is hard to build loyalty. We invest in people; we build them up; and we try to get to know them and build a relationship. That requires a good leadership culture. People do not quit companies. They quit people.

Many employees have checked out but are still at their job. They have quit, in spirit; they just haven't let the bosses know. I have read research that says only about a third of American employees are fully engaged in their work. Good leadership can eliminate the practices that cause so many people to disengage.

People need opportunities to progress. My challenge is to continue to grow the business to provide career opportunities. As an owner, if you get to the point of running the business purely to maintain a lifestyle, your mindset shifts to risk avoidance and preservation. You are not reinvesting in the business. Instead, you are satisfying your own needs and desires. Employees sense that. They will check out on you, and that starts the process of decline.

When you have a passionate vision for your business and you treat your people well, you have laid the groundwork for success. When all of the elements work in concert—your actions, your investment in people, a good leadership culture, opportunities to advance—you create loyalty, and growth happens.

Yes, you must provide appropriate compensation and benefits. But decent pay alone will not endear you to your employees. Management theory teaches that once you pay people what they view as appropriate for their position and industry, money doesn't maintain as much allure as a motivator. You cannot buy loyalty. Good pay must be combined with all those other elements.

The proof is in the pudding. For many years, we have had almost no voluntary turnover in our management staff. The only turnover has been when we have initiated it. We do have turnover among our young, part-time staff members because of their transient nature—they are off to college and other pursuits—but the management ranks are stable. Our passion and our policies pay off.

Incentives

We do have an incentive program for our store managers. Our big goal for this incentive program is to make our store managers want to stay in their store for their whole career. The problem with retail is that everyone wants to move up and be out of the store, and get into the home office, or be in district or regional management. Such a revolving door makes it difficult to build relationships, and as I have emphasized, this is a relationship business.

In essence, it works like this: As the store managers move their sales levels up in increments, we give them a percentage of the profit that the store generates from those additional sales. We have placed no cap on their compensation.

A manager who takes a store from scratch could build it up to the point where he or she has a six-figure income. That is really high for retail-store managers in the size range of our stores. The income could go down as well, but we have some ways of giving them time to adjust. They also have to maintain certain benchmarks in areas they control in terms of cost and other metrics. If they are in compliance with those and grow their store, they are going to get additional pay.

For managers of stores that have been around a long time and are already doing well, the incentive is to keep them that way. If someone inherits a well-performing store, we raise his or her pay by increments over seven years to the level that would have been attained by building up the store. The manager deserves that for keeping up the good work.

Remember, our positioning is that we want to be the trusted authority. The best way to do that is to have consistency in the people and the store, at least at the top. We have created an environment in which the manager adopts this attitude: "This is my store. I am going to take an extra interest in developing my team around me so that they deliver excellent service. I am going to build deep connections with the community because I am going to be here a long time. My community is going to come to know me as the go-to person and the expert."

That is powerful. Our team loves it. Sometimes the store managers get frustrated because they cannot move up as fast as they would like, but we help with our marketing programs. All in all, the incentives enable the store managers to make a good living and provide well for their families. They can feel, in a sense, that they are building that cathedral, an inspiration to themselves and those around them. They truly become ambassadors of our brand.

Chapter 5

BUILDING THE CORE

My cell phone rang as I sat in the airport in Newark, New Jersey, on my way home from a business trip in the spring of 2010. "It happened again," the voice said. It was the regional manager in Texas, and his tone suggested he wasn't talking about record-setting revenues.

"What's up?" I asked. He told me that for the third time in a row, the stores had gotten no delivery of a major food brand. The franchiser had forgotten to place the order. When I called the person responsible, I discovered we were using a completely different process for our stores than the other 250 stores in the franchise. I had come to realize in recent weeks that our approach differed from the national system's in several other ways.

The reality was that we were a growing business with a weak core. In sports, athletes train their abdominal-area muscles diligently. Why? The abdomen is the core of the human body, and without a strong core, an athlete is unable to compete at a high level. The core is crucial to all athletic movement.

We were operating without a core. This was causing extra work and taking our focus away from clients. Our operations had become complicated from a series of on-off fixes. We didn't have the systems in

95

place at the home office either, and the result was we were a business unprepared for the growth that passion and strategic thinking could unleash. I was ultimately responsible for this.

After so many years of struggle, I had done what many entrepreneurs do when the business begins to do well and the pressure is off and the team is growing: I had not been as involved in the details as I should have been. After many years in survival mode, I was tired and wanted to have others take things over. My mistake was that I granted empowerment without vision and clarity of expectations. I had a leader who had grown from the bottom up, was tremendously loyal, and had passion for the job. However, through this process I discovered this person simply was not a good fit for the role, and had not been given the direction and support necessary to succeed. As a result, I made a change by assuming the job duties myself and returned to the details.

This was a painful process to work through. That leader and I both had worked hard to develop the skills necessary to grow to the current level of organization. That person had tremendous gifts and skills, but the fit wasn't there. In the right role, that employee would be successful. This was the experience that led me to search out and implement a pre-employment work profile tool.

Michael Gerber, author of the book *E-Myth*, teaches entrepreneurs that they need to balance working *in* their business, with working *on* their business. It is important to create repeatable systems and then document operations. It is a mindset of being a strategist, holding people accountable, and getting things done. I had done all of that, but in the few years leading up to this, I had failed to follow through on holding people accountable. I was comfortable and I wasn't leading.

So it was time to lead, to make a major decision to change. We would eliminate every store operations process that differed from that of our franchisor. We would go 100 percent on the franchise system program. We would measure operations against the improved franchisor systems that had been proven to simplify running stores. This would lead to us meshing perfectly with the national programs. Before, we had to create and do workarounds continually to operate the stores.

The big payoffs were simplicity, increased time and focus on the client, and better energy among our employees, who were freed from the burden of those complex operations and workarounds. It would be an expensive and difficult transition. It ended up costing us nearly an entire year's earnings to make these changes.

I was facing a lot of resistance to change, and fear and uncertainty throughout our organization. The team had not seen a lot of me in the prior couple years, so I had work to do to develop a connection and trust with them. I had to have a crystal-clear vision of where we were going. I had to believe strongly in the outcome. I needed the energy to carry it out, and I needed to communicate clearly.

The alternative was just to sell the business and move on. Ultimately, it came back to passion. After fourteen years, was I still passionate about my business, our people, and our industry? Did it still matter to me? Was our vision still compelling enough to engage my heart in this endeavor? Was I really willing to tear apart our company and rebuild it?

The answer to all those questions was a resounding yes. I still had the passion and desire to build a great company. Over the next year, I spent a lot of time on airplanes, traveling to share our vision and develop our brand ideal, purpose, and mission. We developed our playbook and the rail. My focus was on building trust and buy-in for this vision. It was during this period that much of our communication system was developed. From this twelve-month process, we successfully managed the change and came out the other end performing the best the company had ever performed.

I was still passionate about serving pet owners. I still believed we helped people have healthier lives, and that our culture blessed our employees' lives. I believed that we had a great vision for our company and that our franchise also had a compelling vision, a plan for the whole company.

In the end, pushing through this difficult period of change led us to getting crystal-clear about what our brand vision was and what our strategy was. I had been pretty discouraged, and I could have given in to it. For the first five or six years that we were in business, we dealt with struggle and difficulty, and we got through that and had several years in a row in which we were doing quite well. We were paying down debt, and our cash position was strong. However, as we were growing rapidly and adding stores, the way we were running our business would have caused it all to fall apart if we had grown much larger.

I had to get simple and clear about what business systems we needed to nail down and tie in to the national platform. That needed to happen if we were to grow effectively. I needed to have a tight focus on a strong operational system. It was high time to get into the details of building a successful entrepreneurial venture.

In this chapter, I will discuss what it means to create the "core" of a business. I will touch on some major concepts that will give other entrepreneurs ideas on how to establish their business effectively.

A business' operational system is nothing more than a set of steps that provide quality and repeatable value to the customer, and therefore results. Those steps can be written, taught, and measured.

Too many businesses operate out of the memory of the founder or key leaders. The problem with that is you cannot scale that kind of an operating system, and you cannot repeat results. Worst of all, that kind of business is hard to sell. The focus is on income rather than on creating business value and long-term wealth.

Every business has a flow to it. You have to think of your organization as a big group of processes or cogs in a machine, and the system I have is a little different from the systems of other businesses. As one example, a business-to-business organization might measure and track every step of the presale, the sale, and the postsale process. You have to think about all of your systems deeply and understand how each works and how they fit together to deliver value.

Map out each part of the process of how your organization delivers value. Break each one apart and rebuild to support the ultimate goals of the organization. You want to measure, as much as you reasonably can, and you want to work from facts, so that your systems work together to advance your brand, purpose, and mission. This is hard work, and it takes a long time and most likely will need to be revisited and improved over time. Doing what is hard is what separates your business from others. It takes persistence and passion.

The consequence of not thinking this through is that the entrepreneur doesn't get to leave the business or to enjoy life, and doesn't empower and train people. This kind of entrepreneur is a technician, according to Gerber. Such an entrepreneur likes working *in* the business. He or she prefers doing things rather than building a business. This person has simply bought a job with all the risk and pressure of ownership. The worst aspect of this style of operating a business is that there is no time to be strategic. There is no time to ask the big questions of why, how, and what is possible. From those questions, which take time and critical thought, come breakthroughs.

We have identified four major systems in our business that are foundational: the client-buying-experience system, the talent system, the marketing system, and the scorekeeping system.

Client-Buying-Experience System

Have you ever thought about what it is like to be a customer of your business? Do you understand each step in the process of buying from your business? Imagine that you are one of your own customers, and go through all the steps they have to take and interact with your brand to complete a purchase. If you do that, you will be able to deconstruct the cycle and identify the key touch points that characterize that process.

Then, you can develop a set of desired outcomes at each of those touch points, and make sure that every employee involved in these touch points is trained to deliver the experience that you want with your brand. We know the key moments from the time clients walk in the door to the time they walk out happy. My team and I worked through what we could do to make the best of those moments. Then we set up a training process so that all of our employees, whether managers or stockers or cashiers, would know what to say to the client and when to say it.

We do not script our employees on the touch points. We give them room to bring their own personality to the situation. Clients sense when words are being said purely by rote. You do not want them to feel as if they are talking to a call-center person on a script.

It is a work in progress. No business will be perfect. But we work hard so that every day, no matter which of our stores somebody walks into, he or she will get a well-thought-out, really good treatment. This also is difficult to engineer, and hard work seems to be the recurring theme here. It takes years to work out the experience you want for your customer. You do not just do this in a day. But in time, you will develop a good customer buying experience, one that is unique. How people are sold to in your business is a point of differentiation. This is often an overlooked strategic option. Most businesses focus on price, selection, product features, location, or the generalized version of "service."

Other aspects of our buying-experience system include our merchandising plan, which involves having the right products in the right place at the right time. We also must be efficient in our ordering, to make sure we keep products in stock.

We pay close attention to the maintenance of our stores so that the appearance is nice. People do not like to shop in dirty environments. People shop up, not down when they have a choice, so being systematic about store appearance is critical for our business. This also includes the steps that take place at the point-of-sale. You can do everything right and then have a bad process at checkout, and that is what people remember.

People do not like to interact with stores/businesses that seem to be going out of business or have a dated or declining look. This is true with a service business or manufacturing company. When I was a commercial banker, the appearance of the parking lot, landscaping, building exterior, and interior design all had a positive or negative impact on whether I wanted to do business with that company. Tired, dirty, and disorganized properties and offices lowered my confidence in management. Clients will have the same reaction. Thus, it is important that an entrepreneur step back and look at the business with a fresh set of eyes and notice the things that he or she has been overlooking for years. I would suggest that you even consider an outside person as an option to review your business objectively.

The first touch point comes when the client walks into our store. Is the storefront clean and uncluttered? Does the client get a warm greeting every time from the cashier, or a stocker, or a manager, whoever is free at that moment?

The second touch point arrives when the client proceeds through the store to the area appropriate for their pet. Our one best outcome here is to engage in a conversation, however we can do that. That is usually through an open-ended question: "What kind of dog do you have?" if that is the aisle where the client is shopping, for example. I train my staff not to push products. The priority is to meet their needs. Most pet owners do not know everything they need to know to take care of their animals, and a lot of people are hesitant to ask. Through a series of appropriate questions, our team can uncover real needs. Our philosophy is that we speak for the pet. They cannot talk, so we use our extensive training to uncover a need the pet may have that the owner is unaware of. We find that most pet owners want to do the best they can for their pet within their budget.

The third touch point is when the client approaches the register. The line should be short. Our rule is no more than two people in line at a time, or we open another register. The front-end people have to be managing that and have their radar up, and the cashier should acknowledge the client in the line as soon as possible.

Touch point number four is the actual final-sales process. We ask the cashier to smile, look the clients in the eye, and ask whether they found everything they needed. The cashier asks whether the client has a loyalty card; we want people to use that for more savings. We also use clients' buying history and alert them to manufacturer offers that fit the pattern of their purchases.

The fifth touch point involves a judgment call. Is this an elderly person or a woman who has a heavy purchase? If so, we offer to carry it out to the car and call up one of our stockers. Most people enjoy that.

The final touch point comes when the client is leaving. We thank the client for coming in. It is that simple. When I buy things, I am surprised how seldom anyone thanks me. I do not think they want to be insensitive or rude. I just think that their supervisors have failed to inspire them to do more than the minimum. That is a fault of leadership.

As simple as it seems, it did take time and a lot of thought to step back and think all that through and analyze it. It must not be complicated. If it is, the employees will not comply.

Similarly, if you are selling to businesses, there are key moments in every step of that sales cycle that you should analyze. You need to train employees on what they are expected to deliver.

This comes down to treating people well and courteously, the way you'd expect to be treated if you walked into a store or interacted with a business. Everyone has had bad experiences with businesses and walked away swearing never to deal with them again. We have identified the key points where we can make sure our clients will never feel that way. Even if they enter the store and do not find what they want, they can still be pleased with the service. They won't feel ignored. I get irritated when I see people treated that way in any store. I know how much better it could be. My wife and kids tell me I need to let it go.

So much of this is an understanding of human nature. It is common sense. It is about what people appreciate and what they resent. People want to be treated with respect and understanding. They walk into our stores with a wide variety of needs and in many different moods, and it takes training to know the right response; it doesn't always come naturally. Some clients are in a hurry. You treat them one way. Others come in looking a bit confused, and you treat them another way. Some want help. Others want to show you that they are the authority. You treat them yet another way.

These are all points of training. You can show your staff how to respond. A staff member may have had a bad day at home, but that cannot influence how he or she assesses and deals with a client. They must not bring their problems into the store. And if a client reacts negatively, we teach our staff that none of us knows what has happened in that person's day. Perhaps the client is going through a divorce, or was fired from a job, or got an ominous diagnosis. Our team is taught to live out our purpose in those critical moments, and that purpose is to make the client's day better.

I wanted an experience for our clients that would be consistent, trip after trip after trip, and it also had to be simple and well thought out. Otherwise, I wouldn't have been able to get the system operating in all of our stores.

Talent System

I cannot say it strongly enough: People are what deliver the brand experience. They bring it alive. They make it human. They differentiate you. The other elements help—paint color, design, product assortment, location, pricing—but they alone usually will not drive the results that you are seeking. In today's hypercompetitive economy, you must meet those criteria just to stay in the game. It's the quality of your people that can make all the difference. Just as you must pay close attention to the customer buying system, it is critical to think strategically about the design of your talent management system. That's what will bring you consistent results.

For many years, our organization struggled to create a solid, stable team. We were guilty of hiring to fill spots rather than thinking of our people as guardians of our brand. That is the way we look at it now. We stepped back and decided to create a system. We started from scratch and asked, "What does the ideal employee look like?" Then we found a tool that profiles the work style of the employee.

It is not a personality test per se; it is an assessment of work style. We applied it to all of our employees, and we found a consistent profile of our best employees. We were able to identify that when we were outside that profile, in general, we had employees who did not fit well for us. In a sense, we were asking people who were "off profile" to work in way that was inconsistent with who they were. Those people, in turn, tended to be the ones we had problems with, and they struggled the most to live out the brand.

When we went through that difficult period of realigning a few years ago, we helped more than three dozen employees leave the company, and we rehired based on profile. Today, the hiring profile is a big part of our talent management system. We rarely hire anyone who doesn't meet the profile. It is now hard to hire. We go through dozens of applications to hire one employee. Our managers complain about that. The good news is that when we do find someone, he or she almost always works out great, and the managers are reminded of why they are going to such trouble. A byproduct of this is that the in-store culture is so strong that we lose fewer people. There is synergy among the staff in our stores. People enjoy working together.

We also rank our employees A, B, or C. That is not a ranking of their value as a person; rather, it is a ranking of fit. Our A employees are those who are fully trained and have fully bought into the vision, and they live it. Our B employees have fully bought into the vision and they live it, but they lack training and experience. Our C employees may be fully trained, but they lack buy-in, and they do not live the vision.

We have a policy that when we identify Cs, we make plans to help them find another job somewhere else because they just do not fit. Our hiring profile tends to eliminate the hiring of Cs. When someone doesn't fit, it is often because his or her internal wiring doesn't work well in retail.

We need employees who are enthusiastic around people and energized by them. That means they tend to be external types. Internal types, on the other hand, are wired to be energized by being alone and working alone. They do not relish being around people all that much. Those people just do not buy into our vision of the touch points. It is hard for them. They cannot make themselves do it. At best, they will comply out of sense of dedication, but they are fighting themselves on the inside the entire time. They find that this is not the way they want to live long-term, and the job becomes a chore to them. A business cannot build brand ambassadors with this kind of internal conflict going on. That is why great companies emphasize hiring as a strategic core competency.

The ranking system and profiling have helped us to avoid mismatching people in their jobs. Those whom we helped to leave—and we did it appropriately; we did not just kick them out—had a chance to find a better job where they would be a good fit.

In addition, we have an online, systematic hiring and intake process. This is nitty-gritty, but you have to do that well. There are many federal regulations on the documentation of new employees, and you have to have a robust system for that. Then, we have the scripted training schedule for the first year; we know what we are going to do the first week and the first month and from there on out.

The next level is the thirty-day action plan, which I detailed in the previous chapter. This minireview between employee and supervisor leads to improvements, month by month. The idea came from a store manager. It did not come from on high in some ivory tower. As a result, all employees, down to the newest hire who stocks shelves, know where they stand and what is expected.

When we applied this system companywide, we noticed that morale improved. It is hardly fun for a manager to confront an employee who is not doing the job. But when things go unspoken, the problem gets messier. Instead, by opening the lines of communication early, an employee's career can be salvaged. The leadership can turn the employee around. A lot of businesses will give up and say, "Well, we just need to get rid of this person." We do not throw people away like that.

We do expect all employees to buy in to our mission, and that includes our young people, still in school. We do not hire just for the summer. We expect any high-school students working for us to train and develop and buy in, or they do not stay with us. We also hire people twice that age for entry-level jobs. We look at them as great opportunities. For whatever reason, they have not found their niche yet. We have known such people who really caught fire while working for us. For the first time they felt that an employer was investing in them. Helping to develop employees was always fun for me. That happens at store level, so I am not immediately involved in it anymore, but it is quite fulfilling to see someone thriving under our guidance.

To further develop our talent, we purchased a training program for our store managers on the importance of a positive, success-oriented mindset. They get monthly installments of that program, in printed materials and a CD. We also have our continuing leadership development program. As new people come in, we develop their ability to think like a leader. In addition, we have the pet-nutrition certification for our store managers and assistant managers, and we have the nine-month, online, pet-care training program.

We feel that we have a vigorous and complete training program, and the payoff is a workforce who fit their roles and feel invested in their positions. They are growing and they want to be with us. We are not using the carrot and stick approach. We hold people accountable, but we do not try to motivate through external rewards or the fear of being hurt or suffering consequences for failing. We aim to create an environment where people are on fire and motivated from within.

When you engage people at the heart level and they are excited, they give you so much more. They contribute a lot of new exciting things and unique approaches to the business, and that is really what we want. "We need all the brains in the game," Jack Welch, former chief executive of General Electric, once said, and it is an expression that we have borrowed. Our talent-management system ensures that is what we have.

Marketing System

The marketing system is often a neglected area for small businesses. Most entrepreneurs are frustrated by marketing. To quote David Ogilvy, the famous advertising executive, "I know that 50 percent of my advertising is wasted. The problem is I do not understand which half."

Entrepreneurs often try to copy what they see big companies doing, and that is one of the first things to unlearn. Big companies do brand advertising, and small businesses cannot do that. The small-business marketing system must acquire new customers who can be documented; that way, you can understand what worked and what did not work.

All of the advertising that a small businessman does has to be tracked, so that you know whether you have a positive return on investment. Otherwise, it is wasted money. Basically, your first-year, new-customer value has to exceed the cost to acquire the new customer. We know our first-year-customer value is based on gross profit on the average, annual, purchase volume of a typical customer.

Knowing the value of a customer, then, allows you to know how much can be spent acquiring a new one. Our goal is to acquire at a cost that is less than first-year value and ideally less than six months of first-year profit. The entrepreneur's marketing either should produce a positive ROI or it should be changed. That is the reason that your marketing efforts need to be measurable and accountable. Small businesses cannot afford brand advertising as it is done by Coca-Cola or a popular beer brand. Instead, you need a clear offer with a call to action that is measurable.

Dan Kennedy, author of No B.S. Direct Marketing (www.dan-kennedy.com), has an excellent way of looking at this challenge of marketing for the entrepreneur. There are three aspects to creating good marketing: what, who, and how. You have to know what message you will say to the market; just who your market is; and how you will get the message to the market. Dan calls these aspects message, market, and media.

You have to understand the "who" first. Once you understand who your ideal client is and know that client's needs, then you craft the message that matches those needs. That ideal client should feel as if you are talking only to him, and that you understand him. That is the standard.

The "what" is your message. You need to ask your ideal clients some questions so that you know how to craft your direct message to them. For many years, I had that backward. I was always thinking about how I could just get more people in the door without thinking deeply about what it was that my clients actually wanted. The result was that I wasted hundreds of thousands of dollars on mass media with no ability to measure whether it paid off. Mostly it did not.

Then, once you figure those two things out, you find the media. That could be a place mat in a restaurant. It could be television. It could be radio. It could be a pencil. It could be a direct-mail piece to a targeted list. You should use whatever media will best deliver the message that you identified matches the person or business that you are targeting. Media selection is also based on the cost to acquire a customer. Early on, what works best are direct mailings such as sales letters, postcards, and shared mail products such as Val-Pak. That is because of their cost and ability to target and track. As a business succeeds, additional media can be added, multiplying the effect.

Kennedy teaches that you should never sell against resistance to your message, which means that you have to be clear on what your message is and match it to your ideal client, who wants to receive your message and respond to it. Like me, most small-business people advertise generically to thousands of people who are not interested in the message. A lot of money is wasted.

There should be minimal wasted effort in your marketing because you understand what makes your business unique. You understand the message that communicates your uniqueness best, and you know where you can find your ideal customer. The easy part, then, should be using the best media to reach your ideal customer at an appropriate cost.

Now that you understand what your message is, who your market is, and what your media is, you need to build a system with four fundamental qualities.

The first is that you want your marketing to be multimedia, as soon as you can afford it, meaning you do not want to just use one vehicle. Over time, as you grow your business, you should use several forms of media because that is where the most power comes from and success in reaching your target.

The second fundamental in building your system is that it needs to be multistep, meaning that you need to communicate with both your existing clients and with your prospects, repeatedly, rather than just once and expecting big results. In fact, most small businesses conduct what is referred to as hit-and-run advertising. Think about it. This is not how bill collectors and magazines work. They send you a letter or bill, and if you do not respond, they send another and another until they eventually tell you, "This is the FINAL NOTICE!" Many people somewhere in that sequence will respond who otherwise would not have if they had not been contacted several times.

At any one point, only about 3 percent of all buyers in a category are ready to buy today. Traditional advertising methods and the businesses that use them are all fighting for that 3 percent. A multistep, multimedia marketing system markets to both the 3 percent who are buying today and the 97 percent who are not in the market today. When the 97 percent become active buyers, whom are they going to go to? The hit-and-run marketer or the consistent multistep marketer? The answer is the marketer who consistently, creatively, and persistently invests in compelling marketing targeted at the ideal customers.

The third aspect is that you have to have a specific strategy for 1) customer acquisition, which is prospecting; 2) reactivation, which is recovering lost customers; and 3) retention, which is ongoing communication with your existing customers. You have to have a specific strategy for three types of situations: acquisition, reactivation, and retention. A system that consistently markets to all three types of buyers produces powerful growth.

Creating a marketing system, as opposed to reacting to your sales circumstances, is the single best way to ensure your success in your business. You cannot save your way to success. Revenues must grow. Otherwise, you will struggle with cost containment in your business, and that makes it difficult to create the dynamic culture you need to deliver a great customer experience.

The fourth fundamental is that you have to create, build, and utilize a database of your existing customers. The best practices call for segmenting your customers into groups, and these groups can be based on any criteria that you deem best for your business. We utilize a concept called RFM, which means recency, frequency, and monetary value.

When we segment our clients as A, B, and C, we do so based on their RFM scores; the higher the score, the higher the letter. The higher the score, the more likely it is that they will respond to our marketing and the higher value they are to our business in terms of profitability. The goal here is to learn how to market to unique sets of customers, within your database, by considering their distinct buying patterns. You do not need to be as complex at that. Simply pick a couple of thresholds and rank your customers as A, B, and C, or some other name, so that you can begin to differentiate them and market to them uniquely.

An example for us would be dog owners who buy dog food but who do not buy any toys. That is a unique group that we can target in our marketing; we can come up with an offer for them to try a toy.

Maybe we can point out to them, in a letter, how a toy can occupy a dog's time so that it doesn't fall into destructive behaviors.

Technology has benefited our ability to become more targeted. Small businesses are able to be more specific by moving to online. When we do radio advertising, for example, we direct listeners to a website where, to receive the offer, they input their name and e-mail address and other information. That way we can track specifically how many people are responding to those radio ads. In the past, all you could do was look at your sales in general and consider whether or not sales were going up. Technology has given us the ability to track response rates on the mass media.

With the help of technology, we can also buy specific mailing lists. For instance, when we send out a sales letter each month, we are buying lists of people who have demonstrated in the past that they have purchased pet supplies. We are not just shooting in the dark at some generic demographic.

Technology therefore helps both with whom you are going to reach and with tracking who responded. You have a much better grasp of how effective your marketing system is through technology. It used to be a guessing game. Now you can see specifically where and how you are being effective.

In every marketing campaign that we do, we can track our effectiveness, either through that website, or through the barcode on the offer we gave to the clients. We can track the response down to the store level. We know how many people are coming in, and we know what it is costing us.

Then we simply do the math. We measure the number of new clients who come in, using the first-year value, and we then divide by the cost. We are looking for a minimum of a 1.5:1 ratio, meaning we received a $1.50 of value for each dollar we spent to acquire them. Often we are able to exceed 3 or 4:1 in this analysis with our marketing.

As long as it is a positive number, we keep doing it. If it is not, we stop and we change. This doesn't need to be complicated. Many entrepreneurs get frustrated with marketing, and a lot of them fall prey to the latest pitch by a sales rep who comes in and sells them on one media.

That is the mistake most entrepreneurs make: They focus on the media first. That is not the answer, because any of those media will work well, if you understand, first, who your best customer is, and you understand the message to which they will respond. Then you choose whether you will be on radio, or TV, or use direct mail, or Facebook, or Google. Any of those can work, but you cannot make good use of them until you understand what makes you unique, who your ideal client is, and what the message is that works best.

Then you have to create a system so that every month you are consistent with your marketing, and it is strategic, and it is measurable. Most entrepreneurs do not create such a system because it can seem like just too much work.

A good marketing plan will be laid out on a twelve-month calendar and will be preplanned months in advance. It will be complex in the sense that it will contain multiple growth funnels. It will have funnels for new-client acquisition, client retention, and client reactivation, and all those aspects will work simultaneously in multiple forms of media and multiple forms of response.

"Know thyself," the ancient Greeks advised, to which I add that you should know thy customers and the best way to communicate with them. You have to know whom you are dealing with, and what they want, and how you can reach them. Your current customers have to feel that you are talking directly to them.

Scorekeeping System

Without question, one of the most overlooked aspects of business is a good scorekeeping system. You have to think about what matters most and then figure out how to get that data into a measurable metric. What is most important to making your business move forward? That is what is often referred to as "the critical inch." You need to identify your major drivers.

We have set up those important measures in each one of our four major systems. For each, we have key metrics. For example, in our buying cycle system, we are looking at our retention-rate percentage and our churn percentage, which are the inverse of each other. The latter is the percentage of clients who choose to not shop with us anymore, and we need to understand that.

Because we know that number, and we know who they are, we have a process to reactivate them. We send something out to them and ask them to come back. We give them a reason to do so. We actually get a good response to that. If we did not know that number, and who they were, we couldn't do that.

We consider the number of A, B, and C clients for each store, and for each of those stores we have goals for the percentages of those clients. For example, let's say a store has A, B, and C clients in percentages of 10, 50 and 40, respectively. We might set this goal: "By the end of next year, we want to move the percentage of As up by 2 percent, and the percentage of Bs up by 5 percent, and have fewer Cs. The more As and Bs that we have, the better and more successful we are. By knowing the allocation for every store, we also know the strategies we need to take to improve those numbers.

This all ties together with our vision and our training. Our thirty-day action plans are how we keep tabs and measure our progress with our people. Those are documented and filed every month. Among our scorekeeping metrics in marketing is same-store-sales growth. We look at the number of new clients we sign up every month. We look at average purchase amounts. Over time, the average purchase amount should be growing, which means that more and more of our clients are consolidating their purchases with us, and not shopping at three pet places. Other marketing measures include response rates on the various media and our ROI on campaigns. On the administrative side, we look at our overall sales growth. We look at gross margins. We look at shrink, and we look at cash on hand, and we look at our debt ratios and sales per square foot.

We actually have individual scorecards for each store. It is planned out by month, and includes those key measurables that we have discussed. We have a master scorecard for each store and that gets evaluated monthly. We talk to the store managers about how they are doing in their key areas. It is a good teaching and communication document.

Facts are your friends. In your organization, you want to commit to learning the truth and to facing reality. To manage well, you need objective facts and measurable statistics. They need to be built into your culture. When you have done all of that, you have provided the platform for accountability. In my experience, I have seen that business grows far better when you are managing to facts and to reality, rather than guessing and doing everything from the gut.

Scorekeeping comes down to learning how are you doing and keeping the figures that will substantiate that. Without those figures and without that knowledge, you cannot know what you really should do next. Scorekeeping keeps you on track.

Underpinning all that, you have to have a very sound and solid accounting system, either with an internal person or an outside firm. Either way, you must make that investment, and you also need to invest in creating an IT infrastructure so that you can get the information you want. A small business can use an outsource company to help create IT and accounting platforms. If you try to save by not making those investments, you will spend more money later by fixing the mistakes you made because you failed to act on information that would have improved your company.

Those, then, are the four systems we have identified. We had pieces of them in place well before the spring of 2010 when we faced those critical decisions. But we did not have them all in place. We were far from where we are today. It was a wake-up call for me that we had grown to the size at which we couldn't operate anymore as a very small business. We had to get more systems oriented. I knew I needed to increase my personal focus and to get into more of the details of the business. It was time to pin down the details and build robust systems in those four areas. Since that time, our growth has blossomed. We have recently increased our profitability nearly tenfold.

You can learn from crisis. It is not the end of the world. It is not a reason to be discouraged. It could be a reason to be encouraged, in fact, because we all should learn from mistakes. We can learn how to do things better. To be healthy and profitable, a business cannot be rotten at the core like an apple left lying too long. You, and those you serve—your clients and customers, your employees, your community—should be able to delight in every bite of the fruit.

Chapter 6

CASH IS KING

I want to tell you about a dark period for me and our company and the lessons I learned from it, lessons that have since led to thriving years for our company. The fundamental point here is this: Cash is the true barometer of performance for a business. You have to monitor your cash and know your limits, and you need to project results conservatively and exceed expectations. Cash is king.

From our first store that we opened in Wisconsin in 1996, we expanded into the Dallas-Fort Worth market in the fall of 2001. We did it all on borrowed money without equity and a cash cushion. Furthermore, we projected profitability far faster than we were able to achieve it, mainly because we had no brand in the Dallas-Fort Worth market. We had put ourselves in a position where our stores had to perform fast or we would be in a lot of trouble. What happened was the latter.

We opened two stores right away. One had excellent performance and one failed, so we had to relocate it. While relocating that first store, we took a foolish leap, and we signed a lease on a third location because we really believed that this was a great location and that we should take advantage of it. In relocating the first store, however, we tapped all of our cash. As a result, when we reopened that first store and opened the third, we had no wiggle room.

As fate would have it, both of those stores opened at disastrous sales levels. We were in a situation where we had an unsustainable ship, and the problem was getting grave quickly. It was another situation that was a defining moment for me. I had a big choice: to take drastic action now or simply give up and file bankruptcy.

After a lot of soul searching, I chose to fight by restructuring our entire bank arrangement, saving us money in exchange for some things the bank wanted, and this enabled me to exit a partner who wanted to get out of the business.

I was able to make that happen. Unfortunately, we had to close the two new stores immediately, consolidating all of our business into the one that remained, but the impact was that we swung from a loss, a very large one, to a profit during the first month after we had recognized all those charges. Now, however, we were saddled with huge debts.

Lessons Learned

Through that ordeal, I learned several fundamental lessons:

- A business must operate with a strong balance sheet, meaning sound debt arrangements at proper levels, cushioned by a strong equity position.
- Never expand where results have to be great quickly, or you will jeopardize the business. In other words, be able to have a less-than-stellar performance early on, and still be able to survive it.

- Develop reasonable projections that are reviewed and tested by others, and then build your debt and equity model so that you can endure a difficult result.
- Put in place a rolling thirteen-week cash flow forecast to closely monitor your cash levels and to know whether you are generating or consuming cash.

Establish a clear revenue, expense, and margin budget, and then compare your actual results to budget each month and take action immediately to correct any problems.

I had violated what I knew was necessary from my training. I had allowed my fervor and my passion for growth to override my discipline. It is important to find a balance. This is why entrepreneurs need advisors and some sort of accountability. Otherwise, your passion can carry you off into decisions that can lead to unfortunate results.

The story ends well, however. The lessons were learned. Our business was rebuilt on financial discipline, and the bank that stuck with me in the bad times was recently repaid in full. I also brought in two wonderful partners with skill sets to complement what I do well, positioning us for rapid growth while shoring up my own weaknesses. It all worked out well, but it was painful. The ordeal took about three years: the year that led up to the problems, and two years to rebuild so that we could think about growth again.

Elements of Accountability

Many of the lessons that I will be discussing in the next two chapters came from those dark days. In this chapter, we'll talk about the components of a sound financial system:

- An annual budget and cash budget
- Key performance indicator scorecards
- Balance sheet management
- A goal management system

The essence of this chapter is this: You need something in place to enforce discipline in how the organization handles money. Otherwise, you could end up in financial difficulty.

Most people are not disciplined enough to do this on their own. We need others. We need outside pressure, and we need measures. In my business, I have a controller who is empowered to question everything and everyone, including me, on any expenditure. I have a process in which I visit our markets and meet with each store manager every quarter to go over each store's performance relative to plan. This is an accountability exercise and a teaching device. Our company also has an advisory board that meets quarterly. I write a letter each quarter to my investors, to whom I have to report on whether we made plan and kept our promises to the board. I am accountable to my board for how the company performs.

You do not have to have all of those elements if you are a very small business, but you at least need to have someone with whom you can share your business results so that you are accountable. That way you will not get carried away with the passion that drives you. Passion, of course, is essential to growth, but it can be bad if it is not in balance.

Those four components of a sound financial system that I will explain in this chapter serve as checks and balances. If you put these systems in place, they will go a long way toward providing that essential accountability.

Budgeting

You have to have an annual budget and cash budget. That may seem boring, but it is absolutely necessary. I get several people involved in creating our company's budget. We do that at store level because that is where the activity happens. How it is done is different for every business. You have to find the natural groups in your business and then create a budget within those groups, consolidating the results into one budget. You must involve the people who have to live with the budget. They need to buy into it.

Revenues are really the aspect of the budget that takes the most skill and discipline to forecast. This is an area in which you can easily lie to yourself. You can find yourself just nudging that revenue line up until it makes your budget look the way you want. You really need to test those assumptions. Expenses and margins are much easier because they tend to be known entities. Where you are in particular need of some outside accountability is with your revenues.

You want to isolate independent or unique business activity and budget profits and cash independently. The closer that you budget to the level of where the activity happens, the better. Your annual, cash-flow budget is really an extension of your projected income statement. This gives you a road map to make decisions on investments and other uses of cash during the year.

In other words, you do your budget, and then from that budget, you create what's called a cash budget with which you forecast each month the amount of cash coming in and the amount of expenditures that you have. After that, it is a cumulative thing: each month, you can see whether you are gaining or losing cash. We use the cash budget to forecast what we are able to spend on capital investments, promotional inventory purchases, over-and-above marketing expenditures, any accelerated debt payments, or distributions to shareholders during the year. When I was a banker, I saw too many businesses that did not do that; when they needed something, they would just buy it, and thirty or ninety days later they would run out of money and wonder why.

Performance Scorecard

The second component is to have a key performance indicator scorecard, and this is your early-warning system. This will be different for every business. You want to create categories that are really the key drivers of your business Dan Kennedy calls these drivers the vital activities that generate thrust for the business. Again, this should be isolated down to the closest level where the activity happens.

We have a scorecard for every single store, and there are only five key business drivers on that scorecard. Still, I know that if we are on track with those five, or most of the five, the store is doing fine. We measure our loyalty-club percentage, weekly sales, gross margin, average sale or average transaction size, and weekly client counts. In addition, we measure eight controllable cost measures that each store team is responsible for. If you get your measures right, your financial results will naturally flow positively out of a scorecard that is performing according to your plan.

I know that if a store, in those five key drivers, is progressing favorably according to its plan, then a lot of positive things are happening at the store level and among those on that leadership team. They are paying attention to the things that matter most, and they are managing successfully. If I see that a store is way off plan in several categories, then I know I need to focus on what that store's managers are doing. What are their daily, weekly, and monthly activities that are leading to such poor results? We do not go in and beat them up and instill fear in them. We sit down with them and ask them whether they have thought about these things that the other successful stores are doing, and we use it as an opportunity to coach and invest in them. Ultimately, they either embrace those suggestions, or they do not, in which case we look to make changes in the leadership. Something or someone may not be a good fit. We may have to change the leadership or change the whole structure of how the store is run.

Balance-Sheet Management

Most entrepreneurs fail to appreciate the importance of the balance sheet. Instead, they focus almost exclusively on the income statement, looking at profits and sales.

A strong balance sheet, however, is a business buffer against disruption in the market and business performance. As a business earns and retains profits, it builds up cash, pays down debt, and over time, the equity of the business grows. Debt management includes ensuring that debt levels are appropriate, relative to the size of the business and its ability to generate cash flow. It also depends on the type of business. The more cyclical the business, the longer and more complex the product development cycle, or the longer the sales cycle that the business experiences, the lower the debt levels should be.

Ours is a cash business with steady revenue and no product-development cycle, so we can carry more debt safely.

Every entrepreneur should strive to build the strength of the balance sheet. It is like a moat around a castle, the first line of defense. It is the protection system against changes in the market. It buys you time to reinvent your business, if necessary. If you drain all the water from that moat (i.e., take all the cash out), you open yourself to risk.

But if a business, over time, reinvests in itself and leaves the money in, and the owner holds off on some of life's luxuries until later, the business builds up these reserves. When difficult times come, and they always do, a business can have a tough two or three years and get through it. It has bought time to make changes. It is hard to reinvent a business in months. It takes years, and the balance sheet gives you the option to do that.

What I want to emphasize here is that paying attention to the balance sheet is an indispensable business practice. Much has been written elsewhere about the many specific ways you can work with your balance sheet. But before you can take action, you have to appreciate the importance, and a good conversation with your local banker will give you the two or three measures that you need and the practices and thinking that lead to building a strong balance sheet.

Goal-Management System

To achieve excellent financial results, an organization needs clear priorities based on the company's vision; a system for achieving those goals; and a means to measure progress and to be accountable for reaching them.

Each fall at our company, we set specific priorities for the following year. Each store manager, regional manager, and corporate staff personnel establishes goals. We have each leader then rank his or her goals and prioritize by A, B, or C, and then assign them to a specific quarter of the next fiscal year. From there, we hold either weekly or monthly meetings at which goals and priorities are discussed. Then we hold a quarterly business review at which each person discusses how he or she did in the previous quarter in achieving goals and what the plans are for the next one. We include an analysis of financial statements for a perspective on how the leaders did in achieving their goals. The focus of the quarterly reviews is to develop and coach leadership for better results.

We have found that this process results in excellent progress and execution. It is simple, yet takes tremendous discipline to stay with it. For example, right now, our company is remerchandising all of our stores and moving our supply from outside vendors to our own warehouse; we are having a lot of challenges in doing that, so we have gotten away from our system here because we are distracted. The point is that you are not going to do this perfectly, but you do need to put these disciplines in place and have the strength to go back to them over and over. They are there for you to utilize, but do not beat yourself up if you fall away from them periodically. We do that too.

The Big Lesson

In 2003 our deep troubles from my lack of financial discipline led to chaos in the company. Employees feared for their jobs, and vendors wondered whether they would get paid.

Worst of all, our clients' confidence in our business was shaken.

My encouragement to you is to be committed to building these four components into your company's financial system. Trust is difficult to build. Other than a failure of character, losing control of your finances is one of the quickest ways to lose the trust of everyone associated with your business.

Fortunately, we were able to overcome this dark period in our company's history and today have all the components firmly in place. No one associated with our business wonders whether we will be around or whether our check will clear. My hope is that I can pass on to you what I have learned so that you can avoid this path to financial disaster.

The big lesson in this chapter is this: You must build account-ability into your business, whether it is through outside people or these systems that I am talking about. You have to have some level of accountability, because when you are an entrepreneur, you are on your own. Many have left big companies to start a business without realizing the level of support and structure and accountability they had. That was a struggle for me early on: I worked in a Fortune 500 bank that had great structure and discipline, and after I got out of it, I realized how much I had taken that for granted.

Entrepreneurs feel an inspiration to make it on their own, in effect going off into the wilderness without the structures of corporate civilization around them anymore. They have to acquire the tools to survive and to thrive. And the tools that work are the fundamental business systems that I have been describing. An entrepreneur may be tempted to bad-mouth the corporate world and feel blessed to be free of the bureaucratic red tape, but those companies got large because someone at some point put a lot of those disciplines and systems into place.

Remember, your goal is to have an impact, and you cannot have one without building a sustainable organization that will stand the test of time. There is a tradeoff, a balance between entrepreneurial creativity and the need for strong and proven systems. When I set out, I wanted to have not only an impact on people in our business and communities, I also wanted to have a better relationship and impact on my own family and church. If I had to make all the business decisions, I would be too tied up to be effective that way. These systems and processes empower and free me to be able to do things outside my business.

You cannot really go it alone. You can have all the passion in the world, but if you are one solitary soul out there, what influence will you have? If you want to have an impact, if you want to do what matters in life, you have to do more than sit alone waxing philosophical. You have to pay attention to the nitty-gritty and surround yourself with those who will help you to achieve your goals. I learned it from John Maxwell: If you think you are a leader but nobody is following you, you are only taking a walk.

Chapter 7

SEARCHING FOR TRUTH

P erhaps you think that you know instinctively what your customer needs, what your employees are thinking, and how your business is doing. I am here to tell you this: you don't.

An entrepreneur and leader must understand that. You must face and embrace the facts, not fear them, and you need to take action based on what you learn.

We have known for many years how we wanted to position our business: we would be the trusted authority. Still, I found myself pondering recently why it seemed that we just weren't making that connection with our clients in a way that truly resonated with them.

Looking for better ways to communicate and market our message, I went through some training materials on that topic by Greg Hasbritt of SimpleWealth Academy. He emphasizes that before you can decide what your messaging and marketing will be, you have to first ask your clients several questions.

We came up with six key questions from the training, among them: "What is your biggest fear with owning a pet?" and "What is your biggest frustration with owning a pet?" We put together an online survey with those questions and sent it out to 1,500 of our clients. We received hundreds of responses back, and we were surprised. For sixteen years we had a mismatch in what we were saying to our clients and what was most important to them.

The lesson there was that, as an entrepreneur, you are not your customer. You cannot assume that you know. You have to ask. If I had measured this years ago, I would have approached my business differently much sooner. We did this survey just in the last six months, and as a result, we are changing the messaging in our marketing, and we are changing some of our employee training.

When entrepreneurs ask such questions, they are one big step closer to achieving the message, market, and medium match that we discussed in Chapter 5. It is through understanding this match, learning to target better, and never selling against resistance (meaning wrong message to target customer) that the business begins to experience exceptional growth.

Not only do you need feedback from clients about what is important to them, you also need feedback in every area of your business so that you can adjust, meet your target audience's needs, and have an effective early warning system if trouble is brewing.

In structuring our feedback systems, we have three feedback loops that we want to be on top of in our business every day:

- the client feedback system
- the employee feedback system
- business operations feedback

Those are the principal areas where you can reach out to learn some truths about our business. You want your actions to be based on facts rather than fallacies.

Client Feedback

Client relationships are dynamic. Your clients are being approached and solicited by your competitors regularly. Your clients interact with your brand, and their opinions, feelings, and loyalty are subject to change at any time. Therefore, it is necessary to have a way of understanding how they feel about your business on a regular basis.

The following are measures or processes that we have in place to ensure we know how our clients feel about us at any particular time. All of these measures are on a per store basis because, again, you want to get down to the roots of your business:

- We have a service recovery e-mail process that allows our clients to e-mail us their problems, and the message automatically goes to the right people, and then we have a goal of responding within twenty-four hours.
- We do periodic online surveys to ask our loyalty-club members a question or two on a topic that we want to know more about, or just to gauge their overall satisfaction.
- We monitor our weekly client count, which is an indicator of how many visits to a store occur each week. The trend here is what is key. Happy clients come back, and as we add more clients and retain more, that trend line should be up over time.
- We also monitor the average sale amount. This is a great barometer on trust level and staff engagement with our clients as well as the quality of our overall store operation. If we are performing well, our clients will reward us by consolidating their purchases with us because they trust us, and they enjoy the experience.

- We measure "churn," and that is simply an indicator of how many clients are choosing to leave our business each month. This is an excellent early warning system. We call or write each one of them each month to find out whether we did something wrong, and we are able to recover some that way.
- We measure the RFM scores that segment clients into groups. What we want to see is a trend toward an increasing proportion of higher-value clients. The opposite means problems are below the surface that need to be uncovered and addressed.
- After segmenting clients by value, we look at trends and work to nurture them into a higher loyalty status over time. If the trends are favorable, we know that the store team is paying attention to the fundamental drivers that we ask them to practice consistently.
- We monitor our Google and Yelp ratings.

That final system reflects a fact of business today: With the power of the Internet and social media, you have to be transparent and address things openly and quickly. Otherwise, clients can communicate with one another online, and they can destroy your reputation quickly if you choose to be secretive and slow in how you respond to people.

That is why we are implementing a system that encourages our clients to rate our service. By monitoring those ratings, we can address any low ratings immediately. If we see somebody rate us anything less than a four or a five, we immediately go into action and are able to contact that person, find out what we did wrong, and try to address it.

Think about your business strategically. Where are your customers communicating? What measures can you put in place to track what they are saying or to solicit their feedback? The important point here is to do something now; don't procrastinate. Facts are your friends, and the moment you begin to secure the truth is the moment your business begins to improve.

The world has changed. You have to acknowledge the fact that people can say anything about you at any time, and you have to monitor that. You must build your business in a way that responds publicly and transparently. If you have integrity and your business is centered on the client or customer, you have nothing to worry about.

Today we are in the process of establishing goals for many of the feedback measures discussed here at the store level. An entrepreneur needs to invest in technology and adopt good goal management practices that result in real and regular actions. You want to review each of your goals, come to an agreement with the staff on the key actions that will achieve those goals, and then train to reinforce those actions based on the measured feedback.

Employee Feedback

The goal of employee feedback is to ensure that employees clearly understand what is expected of them and the level of engagement and morale the organization has. You want alignment around an organization's big brand idea; its purpose; and its mission. You want those on your team to know where they stand and that you care about them.

Employee feedback is a process, as opposed to measures, and the processes that we have in place are as follows—I detailed some of them earlier in this book:

- The thirty-day action plans: Every employee knows where he or she stands, and problems are addressed without delay. This really is a morale booster.
- The weekly store performance summary, written by our regional managers: These reports encourage the team, and by pointing out areas for emphasis, they function as coaching sessions.
- My CEO internal blog: Every week I post a blog about current events in the business. My goal is to keep communication flowing, and I also emphasize what makes our brand distinctive. This keeps me interacting with the team, and it creates opportunities for conversation, encouragement, and teaching.
- Our regional managers meet with each store team once a month, and again go over current events, team issues, priorities, and the brand distinctives. This is another form of coaching.
- I make regular visits to the stores and focus on listening to the leaders and understanding their concerns. I try to remove any barriers that might be hindering them from performing their job, and I also share where we are going. It's another opportunity to share the vision and to teach.
- I have a partner who has a strong background in the commercial-real-estate brokerage world, building networks. He coaches each of our store managers on how to build business so that they can achieve their entrepreneur-pay-incentive program.
- Recently we made the decision to launch an internal employee newsletter to further explain our vision, to share

the events inside the company, and feature an exceptional employee story.

The aim of employee feedback is to keep up a communication and relationship with everyone on the staff. We want to know how our people feel about working with us. What is their level of engagement with our business? It is a proactive way to reduce turnover and improve morale, and you will be delivering an outstanding brand experience to customers and clients if your employees stay with you longer, become increasingly trained and skillful, and show excitement about what they are doing.

When you have high turnover, you have a loss of time, money, and effort. It is expensive for any business. Your clients come in and find themselves dealing all the time with somebody new who doesn't know how to deliver that brand experience. When you have a lot of people coming and going, there is a sense of disorientation that can really stifle a business.

Business Operations Feedback

We use numerous measures to help us determine the ongoing health of our business, and I will share four of those here. The total number of measures we use are a mix of financial, operational, and customer metrics. I will talk about the ones that are the most important to our business. Again, just measuring is not sufficient. When you are at variance with your goals, for good or bad, you must take action:

- Weekly sales, which are the changes from week to week in our sales: the trend over time should be up, and that is a key measure of our overall business health.

- Year-over-year comparison of sales for each store that has been open at least one year: Again, that trend should be significantly positive. Our goal is to achieve a minimum of 6 percent year-over-year sales growth per store as an indicator of overall health in our relationships with our clients.

- Our average client, lifetime, profit trend, which is a measure of both loyalty and how we are relating to the client on each visit. Higher lifetime profits and a positive trend in lifetime profit indicate that we are living out our mission and our purpose and that the client is rewarding us with repeat business.

- The priorities achievement trend, which is a look at our overall goal management system: I consider this monthly, asking whether we are achieving our objectives and progressing toward our goals. All of our goals are posted on our company intranet site, so I am able to see how our employees are doing relative to the goals. I do not personally review all of them. Our regional managers and store managers get involved in this process. But again, if the team members are achieving their monthly and quarterly and annual goals in a timely manner, then that means our business is healthy.

In those four key areas of measurement, the goal is not to be all-encompassing with them. We measure what can significantly contribute to the achievement of our goals. Our people can only focus on so many sets of action, so our philosophy has been to concentrate on fewer measures and thereby be highly focused in our daily actions.

Keeping It Real

You want to know the truth, face reality, and lead your organization confidently to action on the right activities because you have the facts. When you face reality, and when you believe that your actions are aligned in the right direction, your confidence grows. This leads to greater passion. Greater passion leads to engaging the hearts of your employees, partners, vendors, and clients in the vision that you have for your company.

In my own leadership, that has not always been the case. I lied to myself for many years. I assured myself that all was well, not wanting to dig in and find the facts. It is hard work to set up the technology and processes that get at the truth. It also takes a lot of discipline to continually review the information and take action consistently.

I decided several years ago that I wanted to have an impact and enjoy success, so I put the time and effort into creating it, and I continue to devote myself to achieve the goals that I set for myself and the business.

And that is my challenge to you, the Main Street entrepreneur. It is for you that I am writing this book. So many other books are oriented toward big companies. I want to address the local entrepreneur who owns, perhaps, an automotive supply business, or a contracting company in Middle America. I am hardly some guru. I only want to share my story and journey over the last sixteen years and the lessons that I have learned.

I want to share my mistakes and offer you advice so that you can go directly to what works, for yourself and for your community. You can do what matters. You need only commit to doing the work and to listening carefully to what your customers, clients, and employees have to say.

Chapter 8

PSYCHOLOGY
OF SUCCESS

We all think in two ways. Some of our thoughts come moment by moment and day to day. Long-term thinking, by contrast, involves our beliefs about what is possible.

Earlier in this book, I shared with you stories about tough times that my business and I faced when we were not managing our money well and had to pull back. In the midst of all that, I allowed fear to take control of my decision making. Fear can easily lead to thinking small and making bad decisions.

The problem was that at the time I just couldn't see how I was going to pay the bills at home. I made a bad decision. Rather than digging in and making even harder choices so that I could bring the focus that I needed to the business and improve it, I allowed myself to be persuaded by a friend to go to work for him for a salary, helping his business.

I ended up spending six months with him and another six months at another business before I regained my sense of vision about what I wanted to accomplish. Ultimately, I lost a year. I came back into my own business, regained my footing, and really learned a lesson about how easily you can be led to think small if you allow short-term fear to influence how you think.

What I gained was the short-term salary and a bit of money up front. What I lost was time. And I felt drained of some of the energy and initiative that I needed to put back into my business, right when it needed it the most. Outside my business, I lacked passion.

Not only did I lose that momentum, but with my people, I also lost a bit of credibility. I tried to put the right spin on things, as if I were doing this heroic thing to save the company. That really wasn't the case. My thinking was driven by fear.

Among your many management responsibilities as an entrepreneur—and one of prime importance—is to manage your own psyche. It is imperative that you operate every day out of vision rather than fear. So many things can work against visionary, abundant thinking: the market, the people around you, your own doubts. It is easy to think small.

Extraordinary entrepreneurs all have the ability, by moments and by days, to stay optimistic, focused, and action oriented. Exceptional entrepreneurs are not easily discouraged. Their resilience keeps them operating out of vision. That makes them consistently effective in managing others. And that is the lesson: you must master yourself to be a leader.

Living in the Moment

Motivational expert Tony Robbins talks about two kinds of psychology that should be mastered. One is the short-term, moment-by-moment mindset, or your "state." This impacts what you focus on and how you interpret events. Ask yourself, "What is influencing my thinking right now?" If you are fearful, you will see everything through the lens of scarcity, and you will pull back.

If you think out of vision, then you will be excited and confident, or at least convinced that you are headed in the right direction. Abundant thinking will permeate your thoughts, and you will remain on task.

Your "state," Robbins says, will determine how you answer two big questions. The first question: Is this a good opportunity or a bad one? The second: Should I advance or pull back? If you have a fearful, negative mindset at the moment, you will answer those questions in one way. If you have an abundant, confident mindset and are operating out of vision, you will answer in quite another way.

You answer those questions differently based on how you are thinking at the moment. This is one of the tough things about being an entrepreneur. There are so many aspects to running a business successfully. So much can go wrong at any given time. You really have to work on building a habit of responding well and maintaining a positive mindset.

It is critical that the entrepreneur understand his or her tendencies. I used to become fearful and negative quickly. Anytime something negative happened, I would tense up and go into fear mode rather than taking a moment to think and determine what the next best step would be. In the past, that has cost me, such as that entire year of vision and momentum that I lost because I opted for a short-term salary. I have overcome that counterproductive tendency, and so can anyone else.

The Power of the Positive

In our work with Lee Milteer, our company helps our leaders develop a positive mindset. She drives home repeatedly the concept that what you focus on expands. Whatever you think about consistently will expand in your thinking. You give it more of your energy. The implication is clear: you can expand your level of fear, and you will risk failure; or you can expand your vision, which will grow your passion and lead to consistent action toward the goals you have set.

When I went back to work for others during those tough years, I felt I was being responsible, but when I look back, I can see that there were things I could have done to replace that money through a solution in my own business rather than going outside it to solve my problem. I took the quick remedy instead of making some harder choices about where we would spend our money and about the people I had working for me. At the end of the day, the entrepreneur needs to be engaged in the business all the way in, and I wasn't.

Fearful thinking can be more subtle, of course. It can be as simple as pulling back because the economy is bad and all the textbooks say that is what you need to do when, in fact, you may have a business with a unique value proposition, and that is the very moment when you should expand.

I can share that with you. In 2008–10, when most retailers were suffering with a decline in sales, we actually made the decision to expand during that era. We opened four stores during the time that some have dubbed the Great Recession. We looked at this period as a great opportunity because, with retailers pulling back, landlords at shopping malls were more willing to make better deals. After all, we were one of the few retailers that were growing and expanding. My two primary partners, Chad Bush and Aaron Young, are accomplished and skilled real-estate professionals. They were able to go out into a fear-driven market and secure outstanding locations on favorable terms in the midst of an economic crisis. This could only be done from a mindset of vision and abundance, not of fear and scarcity.

"The only thing we have to fear is fear itself," President Franklin D. Roosevelt said in his inaugural speech in 1933, in the depths of the Great Depression. The principle has long been understood: Fear is paralyzing. Just when we need to be bold, we recoil. I have heard it said that of the things we fear, only 5 percent are what we ought to fear. The rest are fears we imagine.

When I became more hands-on in my leadership, I removed a layer from our organizational structure. I decided to focus on people development, on marketing, and developing our culture, all with the goal of creating a unique brand from our client's point of view. I expanded those pursuits until I was devoting four to five productive, focused hours per day on them. Not surprisingly, our results dramatically improved as well.

Typically, a CEO spends so much energy reacting to problems that he or she has little productive, strategic time in a day. Again, what you focus on is what expands, and if you allow fear to control your thinking, it will expand and expand until your whole mindset is scarcity. You are primed to pull back. But if you operate out of vision, you are primed to push forward. You will see opportunities instead of threats.

I am thinking all the time, every day. My subconscious is thinking about my business and vision, even when I am not actively pondering such matters. How can I improve the people that we put out there in the stores every day? How can I improve our marketing? How can I improve our culture? What is the experience that our clients have with our company, and how can we improve it?

As I focus, more and more ideas come to me. I write those ideas down, and then I catalog them by category and take action on them. Action brings results. That is the fruit of strategic thinking.

Your Long-Term View

Most people know what they have to do to get better results, but they do not follow through. Why? As Tony Robbins says, they are not empowered by a long-term vision of what is possible, a "blueprint," as he calls it.

Learning to manage your "today" thinking will dramatically affect what you can envision tomorrow or long term. This is your road map. Not only does it chart the possibilities you see, it reflects your personal convictions and values as well. This is how you see life as it can be. A good mindset leads to abundant thinking. A poor one leads to limited thinking that focuses on scarcity.

How can we foster good, long-term thinking and develop a positive blueprint? The first step would be to become crystal clear about what you want. Do not focus solely on money. Focus on what you know you can be passionate about. Many goals are fine, but vision has to be about a big challenge that engages you and activates the passion in you, to your very core. Write down what it is you want in a series of outcome statements. Then ask yourself why you want to achieve those outcomes, why you want to invest a major part of your life in achieving them.

When I got into business, I had a vision of building a great company and working with other entrepreneurs. I had a vision that I would positively influence people and lift them to a higher level, and I had a vision with an unconventional view toward time. Those "whys" of mine have never changed; they have been strong since the beginning, and that is what enabled me to endure all the setbacks, all the delayed gratification. That is what really empowered me to never quit. I was clear about what I wanted, and I had a strong "why" to back it. I had purpose.

After you develop what your outcomes are and the "why" behind them, you want to develop a clear path to reaching those outcomes. You should take the crystal clear outcome you want and list every idea you can think of that will enable you to achieve that outcome. You won't figure out all the steps necessary up front, but by activating your thinking on a clearly determined outcome, your subconscious mind goes to work on the answers. Because you are focused on a set of outcomes, your actions toward achieving them expands. As you act and get results, more ideas come to mind that you can act on.

Look at each of your outcomes and say, "What are the key drivers or activities that I need to do to achieve that particular outcome?" When you do this, it is best to get away for a day and get clear about what you want and why. Know your purpose. Then, for each one of those outcomes—whether a few or several—write a master list of all the things that you think would lead to success in achieving the outcome.

I keep a journal in which I list the outcomes that I desire and what I believe will lead to accomplishing them. I use that list to fill my daily calendar so that I am always working out of vision and not reacting to e-mail and to the latest crisis.

The process basically forces you to organize your tasks and activities into groups of things to work on. If you started just randomly writing everything down that you think you ought to do, it can get confusing and discouraging. If you break it down into groups and work on each group a bit each day, then you can feel empowered. You feel as if, finally, you are taking action, and that is the mark of all great entrepreneurs. If you are not frustrated and overwhelmed with this process to some degree, you probably are not working hard enough at it. This is very hard work and it takes a long time. If your goals are big enough, then the process is worth it. It comes back to passion. Do you have a real passion for what you are doing?

My point is that everybody needs a big mountain to climb, a level of stability. They need unique experiences. They need good relationships. They need a way to make a difference and they need evidence of growth. All of those lead to feeling alive and passionate. When people are clear about what they want, and why they want it, and how they are going to get there, that is when passion really grows.

Passion, commitment, and focus all come from knowing exactly what it is that you are pursuing, knowing the purpose or meaning that you have assigned to each outcome, and having the discipline to write down the steps and take action.

You must manage your moment-by-moment thinking while also reflecting on long-term plans. When you do, great energy and passion flow. You channel them. You feel compelled to act and follow through.

John Maxwell has a great quote. He says, "If you want to change the organization, you have to change the leader." My encouragement to the entrepreneur is to look in the mirror. Own whatever your results are today, at this moment. Do not blame anyone else. Look at what you need to change and do it. When you change yourself, your organization will change and your results will change. Your dreams can become reality.

A Walk on the Beach

In July 2007 my wife and I were on a little weekend getaway in Mobile, Alabama, at Gulf Shores. The day that we arrived, I got the worst news of my professional life.

My two partners and I had put two years into a major retail-development project. This was when the winds of the subprime crisis were beginning to blow, and a major anchor had made the decision, at the eleventh hour, to pull back and cancel the closing on the land to build a store, thereby dooming the entire project for which we had spent more money than we could afford to lose in predevelopment costs.

Instead of walking away from the closing with a great project and strong liquidity, we found ourselves deeply in the hole financially, without the income to properly support ourselves and work through the consequences of the project's failure to close. At the time, our retail business was still small, with just four stores, and unable to make up the difference. As I sat with my wife on the beach, I was reeling. I was stunned, and I was fearful. I remember telling my wife that I just needed to go take a walk.

I took a long walk along the beach, praying, asking God to simply give me the courage to take one step at a time. My kids were fourteen and twelve years old. I thought of the time, years earlier, when I had prayed by the fireside, looking for direction as they slept in the cabin at Yogi Bear Campground. I had needed courage so badly then too. And I thought of that long-ago vow never to quit.

After a few tough months, my wife and I were invited to Ireland on a ministry conference, all expenses paid. I was a board member of a Christian college at the time, and the president invited me to attend this event with him and his wife.

As part of the event, my wife and I did assessments to learn about what made each of us tick. We learned from the facilitator that my wife was suffering great internal turmoil, below the surface. He encouraged us to find time to talk, and we did. It was then that my wife pleaded with me that I had to get out of my slump and have a vision for us, for our family, and for our business.

I realized right then that I needed to turn around my thinking. I needed to manage and change my state. I had no blueprint, no vision of outcomes to pursue. I was forty-three. I was broke, and I had no income, with two kids. Over the next couple of months, I leaned into my faith, and I put a lot of thought into where I would invest my future. I began to learn to manage my psychology. I re-envisioned my future and why I was doing this, and I prepared a plan to act as a road map to success. My partners and I decided then to aggressively grow our pet business. Since that point, December 2007, I have been 100 percent focused on building our company. Not long after that turning point, one of my two partners joined me full-time in the pet business, and then, in 2012, the third partner joined us full-time.

The thought that really drove me was what my two children would remember about their father. Did he lead himself and the family out of this terrible situation? Or did he give up and place his family in even more difficult circumstances? Thankfully, I chose the right path. During this time, my two partners made similar decisions and contributed greatly to our success in their own way and roles. They too had to manage their state and their blueprint. Thankfully, they chose the right path as well. Today we have an incredibly positive and encouraging partnership. We have been through the crucible together.

As for the development deal that collapsed, my partners and I agreed we would do the right thing and not default or seek relief from the courts. We all got clear about what we wanted and why we were doing it. The banks seemed to find our spirit refreshing and worked with us as we began satisfying the debt that had accumulated with the project. We had our backs to the wall, but we stayed together as partners and now have a good reputation in the Michigan banking community.

Meanwhile, in the pet business, we immediately went to work on an acquisition that doubled the size of our company, from four to nine stores, and we completed that by mid-2008, right before the financial crisis hit. Then, we consolidated that purchase and planned the development and growth of four additional stores that we opened in 2010 and 2011. Recently we opened a new store, signed a lease on another, and acquired six existing stores within our franchise. Thus within a five-year period we were able to grow from four stores to twenty-one.

Managing your psychology works. These concepts resurrected my professional and personal life, and they can do the same for you. You must adopt the kind of short-term and long-term thinking that makes success possible.

What I have been saying in this book is far more than some academic exercise on business management and protocols. All that is important, and I hope I have given you ideas on building systems, processes, and measurements that lead to sustainability in your business. But much more than that is involved in conducting business. It is a matter of the heart —emotions, passions, our human experience—and the textbooks do not talk about that.

Dreaming is more than stars in your eyes. You need concerted action to pursue your dreams, working diligently toward your ends. You must pursue ambitions, and you must learn how to fail forward too. That is where most people give up. They have the passion. They take action. But they hit a wall and quit. They may be on the ten-yard line, ready to score, but they do not know it, and they give up. That is what separates great entrepreneurs from the ones who fail. The great ones never gave up. They learn, as Dr. John Maxwell says, that "failure is only final if you quit." Learn to fail forward and win.

That is why I have shared with you my own struggles. This isn't a book about a whitewashed entrepreneur guru. I want you to see where I screwed up, and how I worked through it. You can work through it too. You are not different from me. Quite possibly the only difference between us is that I have failed more and didn't give up. Through passion, I persevered.

THE BIG PAYOFF

On Memorial Day 2002, I told my wife on a whim that I wanted to take our son, Collin, who was seven at the time, down to Comiskey Park in Chicago to watch the Chicago White Sox play the Detroit Tigers. We are big Tiger fans, and Collin was developing a love for baseball. This would be his first major league game.

We found a section of empty seats to watch the game. After one of the Tigers caught a ball to end an inning, he flipped it up to us, and I caught it. I gave the ball to Collin, and the look on his face was worth a million dollars. The wonder of it all. I told him that in all the years I'd gone to Tiger games, I'd never gotten a ball, and here he'd gotten one in his first outing! The people around us were congratulating him. We have a photograph of ourselves outside the park. That day is etched in memory.

I had read in *Sports Illustrated* that a dad and a son had gone to all the major league parks in one summer. So right there, as we walked to our car outside Comiskey Park, we set our own goal: by the time he went to college, we would go to all thirty major league ballparks. As of the publication date of this book, we will have completed twenty-eight out of the thirty, and he is off to college in the fall of 2013 as a left-handed pitcher on a baseball scholarship. It has been an incredible journey that we have enjoyed as father and son, as well as our entire family. The passion, from the time he was seven until now, at age seventeen, has never waned.

We will complete our ballpark trek in the summer of 2013, when we are going to San Francisco and Oakland, in June, and then we are going to go to the All-Star Game in New York City. I always told Collin I would not take him to the All-Star Game until this journey was finished.

Heidi and our daughter, Lindsay, accompanied us on almost all of those trips. As a family, we have seen America. We have toured the cities and made them part of our vacations every year since 2002. That was something that was easier to do because I was an entrepreneur. I had more flexible time to spend with my family. That is one of the benefits of this journey, and entrepreneurs can strive to provide a family-oriented environment for their employees as well.

Heidi has created photo journals of all twenty-eight ballparks—the experience, pictures, scores, comments. Collin has a collection on our fireplace of eighteen baseballs from games, though Lindsay got most of them using her charm and good looks. At each game, boys line the field hoping that one of their heroes will throw them a ball. With so much competition, it was hard for Collin to stand out. His secret to success often has been Lindsay, a cute blonde with the confidence of a fighter pilot. At each game, Lindsay would stand next to the field and simply wave a player over, smile, and ask for a ball—and it always worked. Often, she also got the player to sign the ball and take a picture.

As I write this, Lindsay is nineteen and a sophomore at Baylor University in Waco, Texas. When she was a senior in high school, she was not excited about her local college choices, not that any of them were bad. I suggested that she visit Baylor, which I'd long heard good things about in the years I had traveled to Texas.

"I could never go to school 1,500 miles from home," she said.

Baylor is indeed far from our home, but she did want to go to a major sports college. Baylor would be such as school; it has 15,000 students, and it is in the Big 12 Conference. However, Lindsay also wanted to go to a Christian college, and there just aren't many Christian colleges with those options.

When we visited Baylor, though, she fell in love with it. I looked over at her while driving back to the airport in Dallas.

"Honey," I told her, "it is obvious that you love this university and you want to go here." She looked deeply conflicted.

"You watched your mother and me make decisions about leaving what we felt was secure and comfortable to pursue what we were passionate about," I told her. "Think about the example you have seen in our lives, and think of all the neat things we have done as a family because we took risks, and unexpected, wonderful things happened. We never would have been able to do that if we had not pursued our passions."

Over the course of the year, she became more and more comfortable with the idea of moving far from her family. Then she went on a medical mission trip to Africa and was gone for two weeks.

"Dad," she told me when she returned, "if I can go to Africa, I can go to Baylor." The separation was indeed difficult, but within a week, she sent me a text, saying, "I know this is where I am supposed to be. I love this university."

She was glad she took the risk, and her Baylor career has been amazing. She's in the elementary-education program and recently left for Europe for the fall semester. Yet I understood how she felt that day as we drove back to the airport, and I think that she understands today how her mother and I felt that day, long ago, when she and Collin were so very little and we set out for a new life in Wisconsin.

There were times when I felt I was faltering, when my wife held me up so I could stay strong. Every entrepreneur needs that kind of support to succeed. Your loved ones need to share your vision and passion. Heidi has endured a lot over the years and gone without. We still sacrifice. We want to reinvest in this business and make a difference, and we have made our peace with that. We are clear about what we want to do.

As an entrepreneur, you need to find such clarity. That is how you harness the passion. When you have clarity of purpose, you see the big idea for your brand. Then you craft a succinct sense of mission and purpose and build a great team that is aligned with your goals. Build reliable operating systems and measure your progress so that your foundation is truth, not assumptions. Build a culture of accountability and action. Pay attention to your financial resources and build a financial moat around your castle that will keep you secure in troubled times.

And there, in one paragraph, is my parting advice to you. Let me emphasize one more thing, because it matters perhaps most of all: Work on yourself. Make yourself into the person who can realize the big vision you have for your company.

You matter. Your investment is noble. Men and women like you, innovative souls with courage and conviction, built this country. Every day, people wake up and go to work and support their families and communities because someone like you took a risk, overcame fears, and persisted through tough times to provide a product or service that we need. You are in the business of improving lives and communities and our nation.

Keep thinking big and always live with passion. If you are going to be an entrepreneur, you must fuel your passion continually. You cannot pull back and play it safe with the focus on yourself to the detriment of your people. I believe that if I take great care of my people, if I maintain my passion, if I continue to take risks and grow the business, if I continue to invest in my personal growth, I will be taken care of very well.

I have learned over the years that those who fight change the most; the ones who are most difficult to sell on a new idea are people who have much invested in the status quo and are afraid they will lose it. As soon as you start to play not to lose, you are done; that is a lesson from sports. Without passion, you fade. My hope is that this book will have helped you to realize how badly you want either to be in business or to get back vigorously into the game and on the journey of passionate entrepreneurship.

An entrepreneur, indeed, faces risk in leaving what is comfortable to embark on something new. "Striking out," after all, can mean two things. But do you really think you have security in your job or in playing not to lose, living in status quo land? Overnight, you can become the casualty of a business decision. I saw it happen to my dad at General Motors. I saw it happen to older employees at the bank where I worked. "That is not going to happen to me," I figured, and I was kidding myself.

At the bottom of your heart, no matter what situation you face, you must be confident that you will have the resourcefulness, wisdom, confidence, and passion to work it through. That is probably one of the biggest lessons I have learned about being an entrepreneur. Dan Kennedy says freedom and financial security are not defined by a number. They come from knowing that if you lost it all, you could go do it again.

Now I am free. I have the ability to be an entrepreneur, take intelligent risks, and understand that if I do get off track, I'll have the wisdom, and the wisdom of those around me, to make it back. We will assess, adjust, and endure. We will not fear failure. Failure is only failure if you quit. I do believe that if I lost everything, I could do it all over again in another way and be taken care of.

So much of success comes down to accepting risk and running with it, not from it. Get over the jitters and seek out opportunity. That is what I vowed that morning when I started the truck and headed for Wisconsin. I did not want to spend much time looking in the rearview mirror, and, despite some bumps in the road, the journey has been a joy.

About the Author

 STEVE ADAMS IS AN ENTREPRENEUR with many years of experience as a banking executive who operates Pet Supplies Plus franchises in Wisconsin, Michigan, Texas, and Alabama, with twenty-one stores and growing. He has been chief executive officer of U.S. Retail Inc., the holding company for the stores, since 1996, when he launched the first one in Appleton, Wisconsin.

"In our stores, it feels different right away," Adams says. "We have passionate pet people who engage you in conversation, ask questions, uncover your needs, not to try to sell you more stuff but to take the best care of your pet. We're about solutions and knowledge, and we also build relationships. We want to be neighborly. We want to help our clients achieve stress-free pet ownership."

Before opening the stores, Adams was vice president of corporate banking at NBD Bancorp in Detroit, Michigan, where his career spanned ten years. He also was a vice president at Associated Bank, Green Bay, Wisconsin, overseeing the credit department, commercial real estate, and treasury management in 1998–99. From 1999 to 2002, he led the start-up of Irwin Union Bank in Grand Rapids, Michigan, as president, and also was responsible for the start-up of banking regions in Traverse City and Lansing. Adams was Michigan president for the four banking regions including Kalamazoo when he left to continue building his Pet Supplies Plus operations.

Since 2003 Adams has been partner with Aaron Young and Chad Bush at Retail Development Group (RDG), a developer of retail shopping centers, with four properties located in Michigan. He has been an adjunct professor of business at Cornerstone University in Grand Rapids since 2006. He is involved in international microfinance projects in developing countries that promote new businesses for economic and employment growth.

He and his wife, Heidi, were married in 1987 and have two children, Lindsay and Collin. Born and raised in Lansing, Michigan, he has two brothers: Dan, who is the company's HR director; and Scott, a Michigan state trooper.

"We were given a solid, middle-class upbringing with good values and understanding the value of work," Adams says. "Our father [Dave Adams] worked at General Motors for thirty-two years in Lansing, and our mother [Jean] stayed home with me and my brothers our entire childhood. We had great parents and a great childhood—could not have asked for more."

Adams is a 1986 graduate of Northwood University in Midland, Michigan, with a BBA in marketing, and in 1991 he completed his MBA at Grand Valley State University in Grand Rapids, Michigan.

Read Adams's *Passionate Entrepreneur* blog at
www.passionateentrepreneur.com

The challenges of being an entrepreneur are similar in all industries. Our community of entrepreneurs can help you grow and be encouraged in your journey.

Scan the QR code below and receive a free educational gift from me. Sign up to become a member of our passionate entrepreneur community.

www.steveadamsbook.com/paperback

How can you use this book?

MOTIVATE

EDUCATE

THANK

INSPIRE

PROMOTE

CONNECT

Why have a custom version of *The Passionate Entrepreneur?*

- Build personal bonds with customers, prospects, employees, donors, and key constituencies

- Develop a long-lasting reminder of your event, milestone, or celebration

- Provide a keepsake that inspires change in behavior and change in lives

- Deliver the ultimate "thank you" gift that remains on coffee tables and bookshelves

- Generate the "wow" factor

Books are thoughtful gifts that provide a genuine sentiment that other promotional items cannot express. They promote employee discussions and interaction, reinforce an event's meaning or location, and they make a lasting impression. Use your book to say "Thank You" and show people that you care.

The Passionate Entrepreneur is available in bulk quantities and in customized versions at special discounts for corporate, institutional, and educational purposes. To learn more please contact our Special Sales team at:

1.866.775.1696 • sales@advantageww.com • www.AdvantageSpecialSales.com

CPSIA information can be obtained at www.ICGtesting.com
Printed in the USA
BVOW031839270513

321629BV00003B/6/P